NAUTICAL
EMERGENCIES

NAUTICAL EMERGENCIES

SEAMANSHIP FOR THE UNEXPECTED TONY MEISEL

W.W. Norton & Company
New York, London

First published in USA 1984 by
W.W. Norton & Company
500 Fifth Avenue
New York, NY 10110

ISBN: 0-393-03285-X
Typeset by Aire Graphics
Printed in Hong Kong

This book was designed and produced by
Footnote Productions Ltd.
32 Kingly Court
London W1

Editorial Director: Sheila Rosenzweig
Art Director: Ken Diamond/Art Patrol, NYC
Production Assistant: Carol Chebba
Illustrator: Peter Milne

CONTENTS

INTRODUCTION

WHEN SOMETHING GOES WRONG AT SEA invariably it is a problem that you have never before experienced, the weather is fast deteriorating and time is of the essence. You are not sure of the best course of action, and you certainly do not wish to be lectured at length about every possible solution. All your accumulated knowledge acquired through reading, study and yacht club bar conversations suddenly seems too distant, too technical and never quite appropriate to the situation.

Nautical Emergencies is designed for just such situations. Within these pages you will find direct responses to a wide assortment of waterborne difficulties. There may be other actions to take, more permanent repairs to be made, certainly more aesthetic resolutions. But the idea of this little book is to give you ready reference...an immediate answer to that desperate question: WHAT NOW?

Obviously, no book could cover every contingency. Hopefully herein you will find what you need when you need it. Every yacht and every sailor is different, and some ideas will work better for one than the other. There is no substitute for knowing your ship, its capabilities and your own. There is no substitute for preplanning and practice, both for yourself and your crew. And there is no substitute for calm, rational action when an emergency arises. That is not always so easy, but every effort must be made to work toward that goal. Too many ships and sailors have been lost to panic, imprecise navigation and hasty planning and fitting out. Think through everything: from gear stowage to passage routes, from emergency water to appropriate clothing, from ground tackle to life-raft servicing. Unlike the moment when your car breaks down and you find yourself sitting by the edge of the road waiting for aid from the local garage, sitting by the disabled yacht is, unless you are possessed of supernatural abilities, not a viable pastime.

Self-sufficiency is usually spoken of with nostalgia. Oh, for the days when we cut our own timber and brewed our own beer! Well, any yachtsman worth his salt must have those qualities but in even greater abundance. He must deal with the increasingly complex and sophisticated systems aboard the modern yacht, whether power or sail. Or, he must keep his ship as simple and basic as is humanly possible, not something most of us would wish to do, if only to avoid family mutiny.

Nevertheless, if you are unable to use a screwdriver, you most probably should not be out on the water unless you are attached to shore with a very long length of cordage. A basic familiarity with hand tools and a proper tool chest are absolute musts. If the mast goes, will the cable cutters be at hand? Do you have a proper-sized spanner to disassemble the head? And do you have manuals for all the major systems and components? Read them now; don't wait until an emergency arises.

Every time you sail from your moorings, you are becoming a pioneer, an explorer. Like the proverbial Boy Scout, always be prepared!

There are many degrees of emergencies. This book is not concerned with everyday advice unless it directly relates to a more serious problem. You will not, for example, be told how to anchor, but you may be given suggestions for anchoring off a lee shore when your engine dies and your sails have blown out. You will not be shown how to tie knots or kedge away from a pier. These are matters of everyday seamanship and should be part of your inventory of seagoing skills. This book has neither the space nor the inclination to cover these topics. When you face an emergency you need sensible advice fast. *Nautical Emergencies* will give you several possible suggestions for coping with any one situation, along with easy-to-follow illustrations. However, *you* must choose the response most appropriate for the particular set of circumstances in which you find yourself. The book can aid and advise only. It won't save you or your ship without your own skills and intelligence. Read it, keep it on board, ready to help when the unexpected occurs. I pray you will never need it.

Tony Meisel
New Suffolk, New York

ABANDONING SHIP

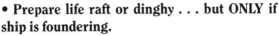

- **Prepare life raft or dinghy . . . but ONLY if ship is foundering.**
- **Gather up necessary extra emergency gear and important papers.**
- **Remain fully clothed.**
- **Be prepared to cut tether only after all crew is aboard life raft.**
- **If no life raft, wear life jacket and enter water from windward side.**
- **If picked up by ship or helicopter, see below.**

See note 1

MOONRAKER MYC

1. If, and only if, the mother ship is in imminent danger of sinking, inflate life raft *on deck* or by tossing overboard to activate CO$_2$ cylinders. Do not attempt inflation below or in the cockpit. Make sure raft is tethered before inflating. In very heavy weather the raft may flip. Do not attempt to right it until necessary.

2. Extra water, food, etc. should be packed at hand in a duffle. Tie it to the raft if possible. Ship's papers, passports, etc. should be in a waterproof pouch, responsibility of the captain. If at all possible, get extra flares, radio emergency beacon and a compass aboard, as well as chart of the area. All this takes preplanning.

3. Hypothermia is one of the surest ways to quick death. Keep fully clothed, including hat and boots. Water within the oilskins will have something of a wetsuit effect, and the wet clothing, especially if wool, will have a high insulating effect. Move as little as possible, only so much as is necessary to stay afloat. Attempting to swim, no matter how strong a swimmer you are, will result in heat loss on a massive scale, unconsciousness and death.

4. Leave the raft tethered to the ship. Too many people have been lost attempting to leap from ship to raft. Only when every member of the crew is aboard should the tether be cut. Take what care you can not to cut the raft also.

5. A dinghy can be used if the life raft is not functioning or if there is none. It should be fitted out before hand, especially with a strong and sufficiently sized sea anchor to hold it bow to wind. However, since no dinghy (or virtually none) is designed for life-raft use, certain precautions are necessary. First, a rigid boat will need to be heavily fendered to avoid damage with the mother ship. Second, boarding will be extremely difficult and dangerous in anything approaching heavy seas. Third, an enclosed form of protection—canopies, dodger, etc.—will be necessary

See note 2

to avoid boarding seas and exposure. Fourth, permanent flotation is an absolute need. To board a dinghy, ghy, be sure to coordinate your stepping aboard with the rhythm of the two boats; otherwise you may step into thin air and descend rapidly to break limbs upon your sudden entry. Do not untether from the yacht until all members of the crew have boarded.

6. If no life raft or dinghy exists, put on your life jacket, and enter the water from the windward side of the

See note 4

MOONRAKER MYC

10

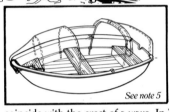

See note 5

boat. From any other point the boat can drift down, or back down or slip to windward, endangering anyone in the water. Keep all clothes on (see 3 above), and assume a fetal position to conserve body heat. A light, whistle and knife should be attached to the life vest. Try to stay calm.

7. Pick-up by ship or helicopter is a dangerous, touchy and frightening maneuver. Inevitably the ship will be larger than your vessel, and the chances of collision and dismasting are great, even in calm seas. You will be distraught and tired. Try to be hoisted aboard, rather than climbing a ladder. Leave the yacht from bow or stern and time to move up to

coincide with the crest of a wave. In heavy weather you will probably be safer in the lee of the larger ship, but you must move fast. Do NOT worry about your yacht! It can be replaced. Helicopter rescues demand even more thought on your part. Clear the cockpit and release any rigging located there, even if the mast goes over forward. Do NOT, repeat DO NOT, fasten the helicopter line to any part of your vessel! Grab the har-

11

ness lowered and as quickly as possible help each crew member into it. At each pass of the copter, be prepared to snag that line. In heavy seas it will be difficult, in strong winds even more so. Signal green if prepared to leave, red if not. Another possibility and perhaps safer is to be picked up from the dinghy or life raft towed astern. However, this makes you a smaller target, and gives a less stable platform for the pick-up.

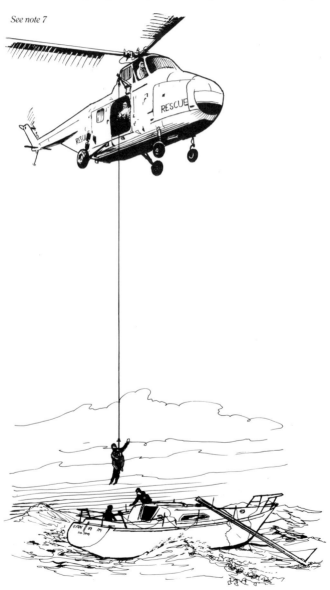

See note 7

AGROUND

- **Determine wind direction.**
- **Determine state of tide.**
- **In offshore wind, back sails.**
- **In onshore wind, drop sails, apply reverse engine gently.**
- **On rising tide, follow above.**
- **On falling tide, row kedge anchor and warp to deeper water; set kedge and apply warp to winch, or with bridle to two winches.**

See note 1

1. Backing sails can lead to accidental gybe. Be prepared. You may be better off dropping the jib and backing main. This will keep the foredeck clear for anchor handling.

2. Onshore winds can vary in strength, of course. In a gale the engine will probably not be sufficiently powerful to pull you off the ground. You will have to set a kedge. Do it carefully in heavy conditions. If you plan to kedge and power at the same time be wary of fouling the propeller

with the kedge warp. Either keep it taut or use floating line.

3. If the tide is falling rapidly, best prepare to dry out as comfortably as possible. With fast ebb and heavy seas you may have to prepare to abandon ship, especially if the boat is on rocks.

4. If the tide is rising and you are on a lee shore, get the kedge out as fast as possible or you may be swept further ashore.

5. Much depends on the profile and

See note 2

configuration of the boat's keel. If a long, sloping keel, you will have less trouble backing off. If a fin keel, you may be able to spin the boat about and reach or run off into deeper water. Twin-keel boats should not be heeled, as you will only increase the draft. In calm conditions, prepare to sit out the tide. In heavy going, you will have to kedge or power off.

6. Heeling a single-keeled boat can be accomplished in several ways: move the crew to the shallow water deck; swing crew or loaded dinghy off the boom end. In a very small boat, you may be able to use the main halyard taken ashore for leverage. (Beware: masthead fittings cannot take much abuse. Do not try this maneuver in a heavy-displacement vessel.)

7. You may be able to reduce draft by lightening ship. Remove heavy gear to the dinghy, possibly drain water tanks. In a light displacement boat, this could decrease draft by the inch or two needed to free the keel.

See note 3

See note 5

See note 6

15

8. Hauling off can be done with bow anchor while crew heels boat. May also be accomplished by aiding vessel. If another ship can help, first make sure that questions of salvage are resolved. Then, depending on your position, pass *your* line to the assisting vessel. Make the line secure first to foredeck bollard or stern cleats with a bridle, or secure around mast or cabin house. Instruct the other vessel to slowly pull you seaward without any surge of acceleration. This is most important. A quick application of throttle could result in torn decks or dismasting. When you are free and able to maneuver, request your line freed. For such tows, polypropylene cordage, because it floats, is best employed, lessening the chances of fouled propellers and rudders.

See note 8

16

ANCHORING

- **Determine the state of tide.**
- **Determine the bottom composition.**
- **Lower the anchor over the bows gently.**
- **Pay out appropriate scope.**
- **Snub the anchor.**
- **Make fast.**

1. The state of the tide and rate of inflow and outflow is vital. In areas of small tidal range, such as the Mediterranean or the Chesapeake, this is not quite so important, but make sure you have allowed for low Springs when assaying the position the boat will take when anchored. Allow for swinging room and for reversal of position when tide changes. In areas of vast tidal range, with swift inrushing tides, such as Brittany or Newfoundland, where ranges can be upward of 30 feet, you will have to anchor far out with very long cables. In such conditions, two anchors should probably be set, especially when tides boil in at as much as 10 knots.

2. Bottom composition can be determined by depth sounder, chart reference or hand lead armed with tallow or grease. The bottom will determine the type and size of anchor you set. Mud, soft sand and mixed bottoms indicate a Danforth-type or plow anchor. Hard sand, as is found in the Aegean and Caribbean, will hold with either but may demand hand setting. Weed will foil a Danforth with ease, and sometimes a plow. Rocky bottoms will be best served with a good old-fashioned fisherman (Herreshoff preferred—if you can find one) or a Bruce anchor.

These two will usually dig past weed the best. If the bottom is mixed—small pebbles or shale, or weed and shale—use a fisherman; the goal will be to get underneath the top layer as quickly as possible. Coral accepts fishermen and plows best, though the shank of a plow can be badly bent by coral and chain cable is almost a necessity to avoid chafe. If it can be found, I have discovered the Northill anchor to be the most use over the widest range of conditions.

3. Too often anchors are tossed, dropped or slung over the bows. By carefully and slowly lowering it you will be able to ascertain the rate of drift, and will avoid permanently damaging the hull, deck or yourself.

4. Scope depends upon depth at high water, holding ground and whether chain or rope cable. All rope cables should have at least 5 meters of chain between the end of the rope and the anchor to prevent chafe and increase holding power. All chain permits shorter scope (as little as 3:1), but can snub more easily than rope. Rope, having great elasticity (nylon) will act as a better shock absorber, especially when in surging conditions. However, rope must be heavily padded—either with patent chafe gear or rags or leather —to avoid catastrophe at the stemhead, roller or chocks. The holding ground will make a difference; the better the bottom, the less the scope. Mud and soft sand will usually hold best, asuming the appropriate anchor. In any case, be prepared to set rope cable with a minimum of 6:1 scope and chain with a minimum of 4:1 scope. Under deteriorating weather and sea conditions, scope should be increased and the possibility of a second or even third anchor being set must be considered.

5. Making sure the anchor is set is the most important single step you can take in anchoring. Either back the sails, throw the engine in reverse or hand snub it when the appropriate amount of scope has been payed out. Be sure the cable is attached to a strong point below decks and is secured to the samson post, cleat or anchor winch. Even with chain cable a nylon preventer is a good idea—es-

pecially as cables have an appalling tendency to snap at the stemhead fitting or roller—rigged from a second cleat inboard to the cable a couple of feet outboard of the stem. Not only can this save you an anchor and cable, but will act as a shock absorber in heavy surge situations.

6. Not only should the inboard end of the cable be securely fastened to the ship, but the cable must be bowsed down in the proper stemhead fitting. In a roller, the cheeks must be high enough to prevent the cable from jumping out; a retaining pin should be fitted, and all metal should be filed down so that no sharp edges are evident at any point at which the cable *might* touch the roller or cheeks. Chain can be weakened by friction against metal! If your roller lacks a retaining pin, or if you must pass the cable through a chock, use a short length of light

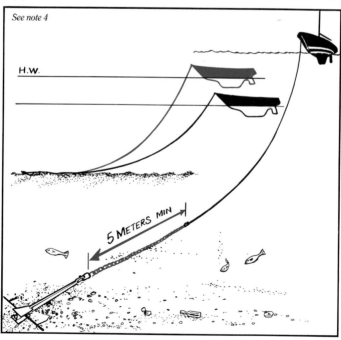

See note 4

H.W.

5 METERS MIN

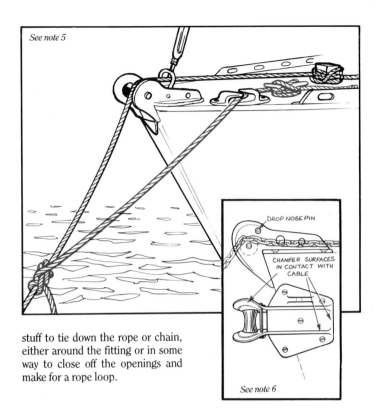

See note 5

DROP NOSE PIN

CHAMFER SURFACES
IN CONTACT WITH
CABLE

See note 6

stuff to tie down the rope or chain, either around the fitting or in some way to close off the openings and make for a rope loop.

ANCHORING: Special

- Changing wind directions demand a second anchor.
- Tidal stream changes mean fore-and-aft anchoring.
- Anchoring in heavy weather can mean another anchor and a riding weight.
- Dragging calls for fast evasive action.
- Fouling demands forethought.
- Trip lines.
- Setting the kedge.
- Short-handed anchoring techniques.

1. When the wind shows signs of veering, be prepared to lay out a second anchor. The second anchor can be the kedge and can be equipped with chain and rope cable. Lower it off the bows in the direction from which the wind is veering. Pay out cable as the boat begins to swing until more or less equal strain is taken by both anchors and the boat becomes the fulcrum of an easy-swinging pendulum, so to speak.

2. In a river where the tidal stream runs strong and will reverse or where there is little or no room to swing, anchoring fore-and-aft is called for. Anchor in the normal way, letting out double the amount of cable needed for the situation—a good reason to carry at least 75 to 100 meters of cable—and set the hook. Then drop a stern anchor and motor or winch the ship forward, paying out an amount of cable to get the ship in the required position. Be sure to station someone in the bow to take in the excess cable at the same time you are moving forward, otherwise you chance fouling the propeller or wrapping a rope cable around the keel or skeg or rudder.

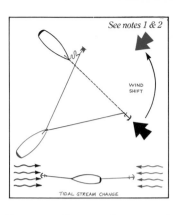

See notes 1 & 2

WIND SHIFT

TIDAL STREAM CHANGE

Be sure to allow a small amount of slack—at high water—in both cables, but not so much as to make for uncomfortable movement.

3. Anchoring in heavy weather or off a lee shore is always a fearful and difficult experience. However, there are times when no other alternative permits itself. Two basic methods are available for effective holding power. *First*, drop one anchor in the normal manner, paying out double the length of cable needed. Then lay a second—much as fore-and-aft technique—bringing up on the first cable. If the two anchors are layed, one

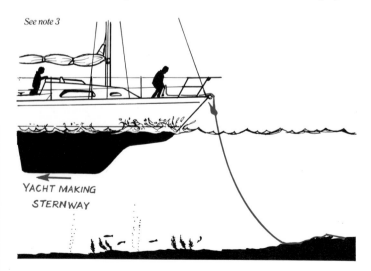

See note 3

YACHT MAKING STERNWAY

to windward and one to leeward, the chances of holding in a wind shift are greatly increased, especially important if anchoring not far offshore in an open roadstead. Lay out extra cable so that both lines will not foul the underbody of the boat. *Second,* use two anchors in line. That is, attach the kedge with a length of chain to the bower ring with a shackle. Lower the kedge first, then the bower while making sternway. Or, drop the bower first with the kedge attached at least the depth of the water distance aft on the cable, certainly no less than 7 to 8 meters distance. Remember, in any storm situation the strains on deck attachment points will be excessive. Make sure that chain cable can be released instantly if you must drop the anchor and run. Buoy the chain before releasing it.

4. Dragging can be much more than a nuisance. On a lee shore it can be deadly. If your boat begins to drag—something you can tell from reference to landmarks—start the engine first! Then pay out more cable. If this does not work, motor up, taking in cable and reset the anchor. If the bottom is suspect, try running a riding weight down the anchor cable. This can be a patent device or a ball of chain. Just make sure that what-

ever weight you use is reasonably heavy, say equal to the weight of the kedge anchor. If this does not work effectively, set a second anchor at an angle of 25 to 35 degrees.

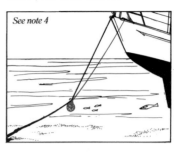

See note 4

5. There are times when you will foul the anchor, either on seabed refuse or underwater cables or with another anchor. First, try hauling in cable until it is vertical and taut. Then move weight aft to try breaking it out or supply appropriate leverage via a windlass. If this doesn't work, try sailing or motoring out, pulling in the opposite direction from which the anchor was originally set. So much for the easy methods. All the rest take a certain amount of real and imaginary labor. You can run a loop of line or chain down over the anchor cable, carry it out in the dinghy and then haul from the opposite

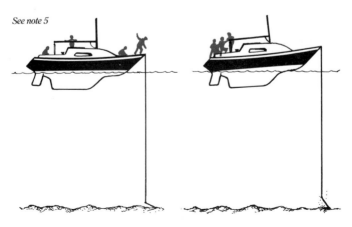

See note 5

See note 5

22

direction. Or, you can use a grapnel (or a small hook as such) from the *anchored* dinghy to try and pick up the main anchor, or any obstructing cable. Needless to say, a member of the crew must be stationed at the bow of the mother ship and at its wheel to cover any possibility of backward drift. If the anchor and cable are fouled by another boat's ground tackle, attempt to raise both anchor *and* cable, securing it by a line to the boat as you lift the pair higher and higher. Then try to free the anchor by hand from the dinghy (tethered to the mother ship).

6. When the chance exists that you will be in a crowded anchorage (what isn't these days?) or expect that you shall have to depart an anchorage with greater dispatch than you had perhaps originally planned, it is a good idea to set up a buoyed trip line. Very simply, attach a length of reasonably light cordage (8mm) to the crown of the anchor before lowering it. To the "top" end, tie a short length of chain to steady it and a small buoy or plastic bottle. This will tend to keep other boats away; should the anchor become fouled, it will give you a ready-set method for breaking it free.

7. If you single-hand, setting an anchor can be a frantic experience. First, lower and secure the mainsail. You will find it much easier to handle

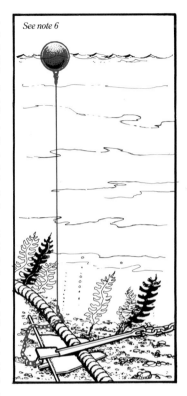

See note 6

the boat under just foresail and without the danger of swinging booms and backing sails. Pass the rode or cable outside of all stanchions and lines aft to the cockpit, making sure the cable is secured, with the necessary scope, to the foredeck. You can release both anchor and jib sheets

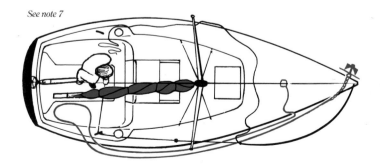

See note 7

23

together, calmly move forward and snub anchor and lower the jib one after the other. Release latches to drop the anchor from a roller chock are not to be recommended. They have a tendency to stick or you may release the anchor and accidentally overshoot the rode, creaating a large tangled mass about the underwater appendages of your boat.

BOOM BREAKS

• Use flat-sided splints—floorboards, fiddles, bunk boards—lashed to either side of boom extending a couple of feet beyond break either side.
• If the boom is shattered or fractured beyond repair, remove it and lash a spinnaker pole, boat hook or such to the gooseneck, with the mainsail reefed. Tie reef points around jockey boom.
• If the gooseneck ruptures, lash inboard end of boom to mast using reefing hooks or any projection. Apply chafe protection.
• If all else fails, and you must sail without a boom, reinforce the clew and lead separate sheets to the quarters, then forward to winches by way of the spinnaker turning blocks; or, in desperation, bend sheets to clew fitting, lash around the clew corner and lead as above.
• Set storm trysail.

See above

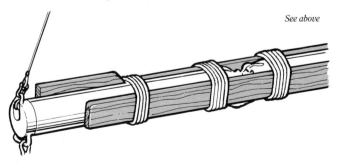

1. If foot or mainsail leads into a groove in the boom, lashing will be next to impossible, using splints. Try a boomless approach.

2. If using a substitute boom, be sure to reef the mainsail. The stress on the clew will be great and you stand a good chance of ripping the clew fitting out if you do not spread the strains along the foot by tying off reef points.

3. Lashing a boom to the mast without benefit of the gooseneck is a dangerous and never-easy job. Drop the main immediately, tie down

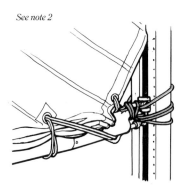

See note 2

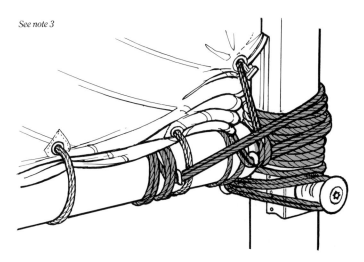

See note 3

boom to prevent damage to boat and crew. Use several heavy lashings tied off independently of one another. Apply as much chafe protection as possible, especially to the inboard end of the boom.

4. Boomless jury-rigged mains are no laughing matter. You may destroy the sail without proper reinforcement. Sail shape will be distorted, and the forces on the clew will be extreme. Leads can be either to turning blocks or snatch blocks on the rail. Remember that the forces are doubled and the snatch blocks and

See note 4

See note 4

their deck attachment points must be massively robust.

5. Storm trysails are remarkably efficient, rarely used sails. You should, of course, know how to set one, and have it in readiness and good repair with its sheets attached. Since it is designed to be used boomless, you have, in your sail locker, the perfect solution to a broken boom.

See note 5

CHAFE

• If badly chafed and in danger of letting go, cut line and join ends by a sheetbend or two bowlines.
• If chafe is at point where the line passes through a sheave, reverse line end-for-end.
• To avoid chafe, pad line by various methods (see below).
• Cut and splice.

See note 1

1. A sheetbend is the quickest way to take care of serious chafe, though it must be remembered that knots will never be as strong as the original or as a splice. Using two bowlines will have the advantage of easy undoing of the knots no matter how heavy the strain on the lines.
2. The easiest thing to do is to end-for-end the line, although, depending on the application, this can cause further chafe and weakening of the line. However, with modern fiber rope this is rarely a problem, and top-quality polyester rope will last as long as twenty years with proper care. Better, get rid of the original cause of the chafing: unfair leads, rough edges (especially on metal fitting, the application of a fine-toothed file will achieve wonders), and so on.

See note 3

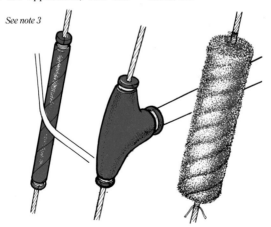

3. Padding—whether by plastic tubing or hose, rags, leather, a sacrificial rope whipping or baggywrinkle—is as old a practice as the sailor has. Where sail chafe is involved, the best recourse is to have the sail recut or reinforced. Baggywrinkle is ugly, soils the sails, and creates a surprising amount of windage. Better is to use shroud rollers or spreader tips. No matter what method is chosen, the padding must be secured, either with tape or whipping.

4. The most secure method of repairing a chafed line, short of replacing the line altogether, is to cut and splice it. A short splice will be stronger, but will not be able to pass through a block sheave; a long splice will be close to the original diameter of the line and will pass, providing the sheave is large enough in the first place.

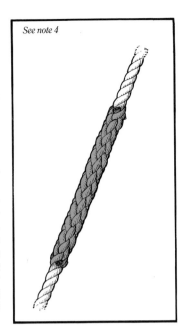

See note 4

COLLISION

- **Take a series of bearings.**
- **Signal appropriately.**
- **Take evasive action.**

See note 4

1. If bearings remain constant, chances are you are on a collision course. Taking bearings at night can be especially difficult. Try to keep one set of the approaching ship's range lights in line.

2. Chances are that a large ship will not spot you until after you have spotted her. You will probably have to take evasive action, but you should attempt to signal first:

5 or more short blasts of a

horn will be taken as a warning. At night, either 5 short flashes of a strong light, or the Morse code "U" (2 short and 1 long flashes). Also, a torch shown against the sails or a white flare will indicate your presence.

Warning signals:

One blast: I am altering course to starboard.

Two blasts: I am altering course to port.

Three blasts: I am going astern.

Five blasts: Watch out! *or* I do not comprehend your intentions or actions.

3. Evasive action does not mean sailing until you see the whites of their eyes! Make all maneuvers with decision and positively. Course changes should be large and the new course should be held. Do NOT constantly change course; you will only confuse the oncoming ship. Always try to pass astern of the approaching vessel.

4. Despite all the rules of the road, you should not hold to etiquette. Forget everything you ever learned about sail over power, etc. You should be the one to avoid the other vessel. Especially with large ships at sea, not always, but often, the watch will be short-handed or they will not be manning the radar, in particular with flag-of-convenience registry. Right of way is only of import if the other vessel responds in kind; otherwise, assume she is going to make mincemeat of you and act accordingly. If there is a chance of a head-on collision, both vessels SHOULD alter their courses to starboard. If the other does not, take immediate evasive action, under the fastest means possible, full throttle ahead.

5. If a collision is unavoidable, try to present the smallest area of your ship as is possible to the oncoming vessel. This will, hopefully, lessen the impact and the resultant damage. If you are struck, the other vessel—if a large tanker, say—may not even know she has hit you. Get off distress flares as fast as possible. Sound horns, bells, sirens—anything to attract attention. Have the crew stand by to abandon ship.

See note 5

DINGHY

- **Don't overload!**
- **Step in to the center.**
- **Row appropriately.**
- **Launch and retrieve with care.**

See note 1

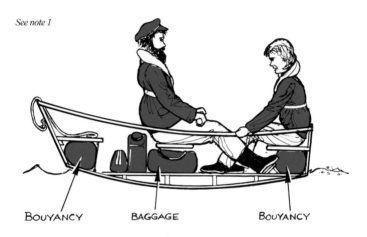

BOUYANCY   BAGGAGE   BOUYANCY

1. More deaths are probably caused by swamped and capsized dinghies than by anything else on the water. The average tender is perhaps 8 or 10 feet in length and cannot really hold more than three people in anything but a dead calm. In truly rough water, no more than two should attempt a journey. As well as not overloading with people, you must be careful to avoid masses of gear, especially in the ends of the boat. Try to keep the boat carefully trimmed and balanced, both athwartships and fore-and-aft.

2. The novice will inevitably step on the gunwale when trying to board. This can lead to lacerations or a dunking. In most hard tenders, you can step directly into the center portion of the floorboards. However, if the dock or float is particularly high, you may have to alight on the center thwart and descend quickly. The idea is to sit down as quickly as possible, whilst the next crew member comes aboard. NEVER board a dinghy with your hands full. Either load first, or enter and have someone else hand the cargo to you once you are seated.

3. Most dinghy oars are far too

See note 2

short, too heavy and ill-balanced. Ideally, they should fit into the tender, be made of spruce and shaped to be comfortable to use and efficient at propelling the boat. Far too few people ever bother to learn to row properly. The beamier the boat, the shorter the strokes; the heavier the seas, the shorter the strokes is a fairly sound rule of thumb. However, load, windage, sea state, wetted surface all play a part in the best (read: most effective, least tiring) way to row. Practice. And be sure that you have oarlocks, leathers and a rowing position—with foot brace—that can stand up to the job. Trial and error will find the way.

4. Getting the dink into the water and back on board is the first concern of the cruising sailor. It must always be tethered to the mother ship. Too often a perfect launch is followed by a perfect drift into the distance. Obviously, the method of launching is dependent upon the ship, but usually some sort of hoist and tackle arrangement will be necessary to accomplish the job with minimum fuss and danger. Always try to have an extra hand to assist. Probably the greatest danger—other than overloading—is in landing or launching through surf. This is NEVER a deed to be undertaken lightly! With oar power, the difficulty will be to restrain the dinghy enough or propel it fast enough. With an outboard, the problems are stalling, cavitation and general unreliability if swamped. And that is the danger: swamping, or capsize. If the surf is running with any power, you would be well advised to stay on the ship or beach. Otherwise, you shall need a large enough boat and crew to power through. Do not underestimate the power of breaking seas. They can crack your boat into pieces and kill you and your crew.

See note 4

DISMASTING

- If the mast breaks at or near the base, it will go overboard; it must be secured or cut loose.
- If the forestay parts whilst beating, the mast can fracture and fall aft into the cockpit.
- If the mast breaks at the spreaders, it must be untangled and a jury rig set.
- No matter what, IMMEDIATE ACTION will be necessary!

See note 1

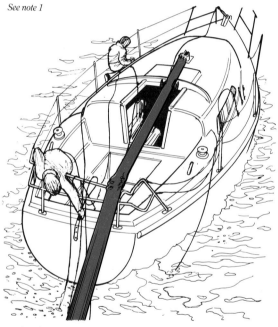

1. A mast that has gone overboard presents a serious threat to the continuing integrity of the hull, especially in heavy weather. In calm seas, you and the crew may be able to hoist the mast back on board. If the mast is sizeable and therefore heavy, a better procedure will be to lash it to the hull. Hoisting will necessitate securing the spar on at least three points along its length, and rigging tackles fore, aft and amidships—using winches in the cockpit, perhaps the vang to the maststep and the anchor windlass with appropriate jury-rigged fairleads. Station crew at each location and be sure that the hull is appropriately fendered; in this in-

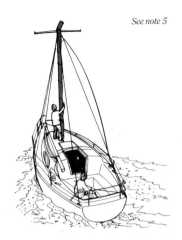

See note 5

masts, unless foam-filled, will sink fairly quickly. It is imperative to move with dispatch.

2. If you decide to lash the mast to the side of the yacht, a large part of the rigging will have to be cut away. This can be done either by undoing the rigging screws (which shall most likely be bent out of shape by the shock) or by cutting the rigging wires, either with cable cutters or with a cold chisel and hammer against a steel block. Be warned: rod rigging will not be so easy to part. That rigging which can be left— lower shrouds on the side of the vessel on which the mast went over— should be kept as added security. Remember, however, that it may be necessary, in increasing heavy weather, to cut the mast adrift. Those remaining attachment points will hamper any efforts to do so.

3. An additional thought: the mast can be left trailing from bow or stern to act as a sea anchor. In truly atrocious seas, this may well be the best way to retain some steerage and control. This must be accompanied by

stance, every fender aboard should be secured to the rail on the hoisting side. Chances are that the lifelines and stanchions went by the board when the mast went over, so safety harnesses are *de rigeur*. Since most masts will add considerable weight to the side to which they have been lashed, it may be necessary, especially in a light-displacement boat, to rearrange the stores and weights below deck. In addition, metal

See note 2

constant watch, for the errant spar could well be flung onto the ship by breaking seas. In such a case, the mast should be secured with rope cordage, rather than by rigging wire, since cutting it loose if necessary will be much simplified if an axe can take precedence over a pair of cutters.

4. Should the mast fall aft, chances are crew in the cockpit will be injured, wheel or tiller will be broken, the cabin house may fracture. Get any injured crew below and commence appropriate first aid. The mast should probably be cut away as soon as possible. If the steering mechanism is broken see JURY RUDDER, BROKEN TILLER, etc.

5. Breaks at the spreaders are more common than one would wish to imagine. Due to the number of fittings, terminals, etc., at that point, the mast can be weakened. If the mast should fracture and the upper portion come tumbling down, lash it to deck and proceed to JURY RIGS. If the mast is left dangling, lash the upper part to the portion left standing; trying to cut down the top and maneuver it to the deck can be a tricky and dangerous job.

6. Move fast to avoid damage to the ship, but not so fast as to endanger the crew. Think out your actions first and instruct the crew carefully and clearly on what must be done.

See note 3

DIVING

- **Anchor or heave to.**
- **Secure the person diving with a line.**
- **Arrange signals.**
- **Always have someone standing by on deck.**

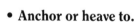

1. Attempting to dive when the boat is in motion is foolhardy in the extreme. Any additional movement will make any underwater task extraordinarily difficult for the diver. The most usual reason for having to dive is either to unfoul the anchor or to clear the propeller. In either case BE SURE THE IGNITION IS OFF!

2. Since few people can remain underwater without artificial breathing apparatus for more than 45 seconds to one minute, especially when exerting themselves, a safety line is a must. The person on deck should have prearranged signals with the diver: one jerk on the line, pull up; two jerks, help; etc.

3. A line without a tender is useless. The person on deck will often sight danger before the diver: shark approaching, squall coming, etc.

4. Always have a boarding ladder secured before the diver goes in. He will know where it is and there will be no fumbling when it is needed. Make it as long as possible and weight the bottom rung.

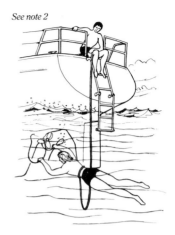

See note 2

See note 4

DOCKING

- **Approach with caution.**
- **Have all lines and fenders prepared and correctly positioned.**
- **Be prepared to change side of approach quickly.**

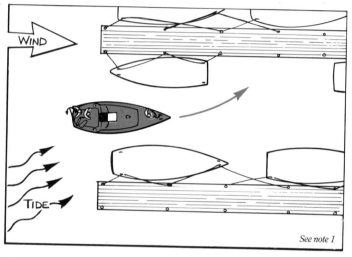

See note 1

1. Approaching any dock or quay or pontoon is made more difficult by the tight quarters, proximity of other vessels and the tricks tidal streams can play amongst pilings and walls. Make due allowance for windage, drift and lost control at low speeds. Know how your ship handles! Attempt to approach to windward. With wind and tide behind you, you will have to either play with bursts of reverse on the throttle or have a crew member stationed to drop a stern anchor to slow down the ship and allow for some control. The same maneuver can be practiced with current abeam.

2. Cleat all lines and pass through chocks, then outboard and over any rails or lifelines. Secure all fenders overboard. If approaching a concrete or stone pier, use fenderboards. Quite often the pier will be quite high; a crew member should be stationed so he can scale the wall (hopefully by ladder) with both bow *and* stern lines in hand. The same is true if sailing alone or with one crew. Spring lines can be rigged after bow and stern are secured. Should the ship be tied up on the windward side of the dock, a kedge can be run out to hold it off, either from a spring cleat amidships or with two warps leading from the kedge to both bow and stern cleats.

See note 2

HEAVE II

3. You could suddenly have to alter your intended approach or goal, either due to the unexpected appearance of a smaller, hitherto unseen boat, or to directions from the dockmaster. Lines, fenders, etc., will have to be quickly switched. If you have enough time, it pays to back off and reapproach *after* these chores have been completed. If not, and the area is crowded on first approach, it is a good idea to rig lines and fenders on both sides of the yacht. In places like St. Peter Port or Newport or Annapolis, at the height of the season, docking is always at a premium. Plan accordingly.

4. In most of the Mediterranean, tying up stern-to is the norm. This is accomplished by letting out the best bower about 100 feet (30 m) plus the length of the ship from the quay and backing toward the dock. Unfortunately, with adverse conditions this can be at best a tricky maneuver. Better to drop the hook from the stern and go in bow first. Most boats have greater control in forward, as well as greater stopping power. In addition, should you desire such things, your privacy will be that much more. If you wish you can end-for-end the bow and anchor lines—providing there is room port and starboard—and turn the ship

See note 2

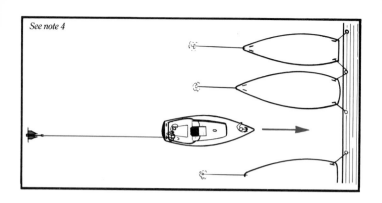

See note 4

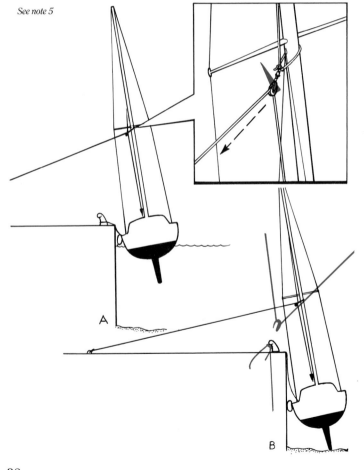

See note 5

A

B

around. If boats are wedged in on both sides, extend the line to the quay and haul well clear of your neighbors before attempting to make the turn.

5. Should the berth be one that dries out at low tide, attempt to heel the boat slightly inward toward the quay. A line passed about the mast at spreader height and led ashore will usually do the trick. Be careful that the rigging does not come in contact with the dock, and that the spreaders will not be damamged. A block attached to a halyard and also held around the mast with a strop or loose loop of rope can be hoisted aloft to just below the spreaders AFTER a line from the dock has been led through it and back to the dock or to a cleat on deck. In addition, a heavy anchor can be placed on the dockside deck of the vessel.

6. Be sure in any tidal area that enough slack is kept in the docking line to allow for the rise and fall of the ship. A good idea is to lead the lines to the dock pilings or cleats in a bight and then back again to the deck cleats. In this manner, you will be able to make adjustments without leaving the deck.

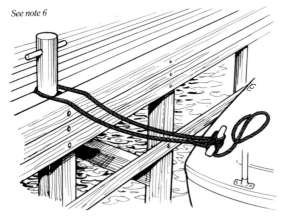

See note 6

ELECTRICS

- **Lights fail.**
- **Engine won't start.**
- **No power at all!**

1. It is a sorry fact of life afloat that sooner or later salt air and moisture will have a detrimental effect on you boat's electrical system. You can guard against run-of-the-mill failure by checking all connections, wiring, fuses, junction boxes, circuit breakers, battery installations, etc., at the commencement of every season and at least twice during the course of the season. Battery terminals must be cleaned and, after reconnecting, coated with a thin layer of grease (waterproof). Check all wire clips to see that no breaks have occurred in the insulation. Any wires running low in the ship, especially in the bilges, should be rerouted away from any possible water contamination. Overhaul the alternator and generator. Replace all fuses and lamp bulbs as a matter of course. See that all connections and connecting clips are free from corrosion and coated after cleaning and reassembly. Top up batteries and secure. Make sure they are properly vented. Check engine wiring harnesses and make sure all wires are securely clipped and away from any excessive heat sources.

2. Assuming you have done all the above and the power fails, what do you do? First check the battery. It may be dry. A connection may be vibrated or torn loose. The alternator may not be functioning. A fuse may be blown, or a cable may have shorted out.

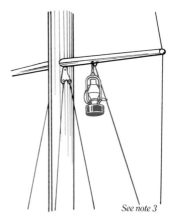

See note 3

3. Having checked the above, and found the situation beyond repair, the following are all reasonable alternatives:

Use a kerosene/paraffin lantern hung in the rigging instead of navigation lights. At worst you will be thought a fisherman! Or use an electric/battery anchor light.

If the engine has no hand-crank starting capability, and a second battery is available, jump or reconnect the cables. Sail.

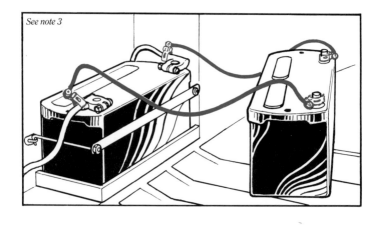

See note 3

ENGINE FAILURE: Diesel

- **Engine stops.**
- **Engine is overheating.**
- **Oil pressure drops.**
- **Engine runs unevenly.**
- **In all the above cases, STOP ENGINE!**

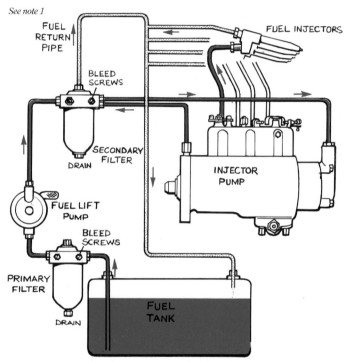

See note 1

FUEL
RETURN
PIPE

FUEL INJECTORS

BLEED
SCREWS

SECONDARY
FILTER
DRAIN

INJECTOR
PUMP

FUEL LIFT
PUMP

BLEED
SCREWS

PRIMARY
FILTER

FUEL
TANK

DRAIN

1. If the engine stops on its own accord, switch off the ignition. Check the fuel system. Filters must be free of dirt and water. They should be filled with oil. The possibility exists that the tanks are empty. The filters may be only partly filled if this is the case. However, partial filter filling may also be due to a fuel line blockage. If the engine won't restart, you will have to bleed both filters and possibly injectors. Consult your owner's manual.

2. Overheating is the most common problem with diesels and is most often the result of a torn or failed water-cooling pump impeller. First, though, check the water inlet for debris and blockage. Also check the belt to the water pump and make

See note 2

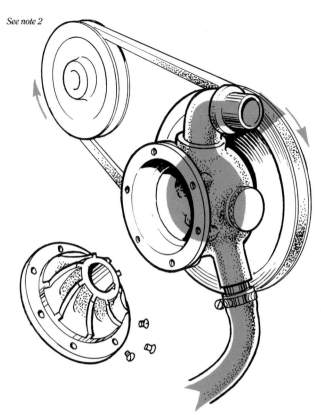

sure the propeller is not fouled. This is the place to warn you: ALWAYS CARRY A SPARE IMPELLER. Changing it is a ten-minute job at most, but for want of a spare, you may be disabled until you can signal for a tow (in a powerboat) or the breeze picks up.

3. Oil pressure dropping can indicate a major problem. Check the oil level and top up. If water has mixed with the oil, the head gasket may have ruptured. Do not run the engine above very low rpms (no higher than 1500 rpm in most modern marine diesels).

4. If the engine will not start, yet the starter motor is turning over, the glow plug may need replacement.

5. Uneven running may be due to a clogged or broken injector. If possible, replace; if not, run engine very slowly.

6. A full spare kit as well as the manufacturer's manual should be aboard for anything more than a day sail. Read the manual before setting out on a cruise. Make sure you have the necessary tools on board. As mentioned above, should anything seem wrong—high temperature, rough running, frequent stoppages, oil pressures fluctuations—STOP THE ENGINE IMMEDIATELY! Failure to do so may cause major damage. Remember that anything that moves needs maintenance. As much as you might hate the "iron jib," it is part of the yacht and needs the same care as the brightwork and winches.

ENGINE FAILURE: Gas/Petrol

- **Engine will not start.**
- **Engine stops.**
- **Engine is overheating.**
- **Oil pressure drops.**
- **Engine runs unevenly.**

See note 1

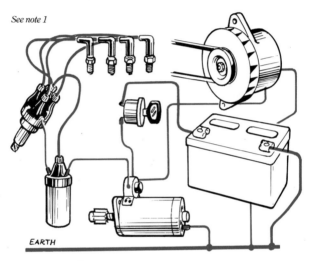

EARTH

1. Check the electrical system. The battery may be dead, especially if the starter motor will not turn over. A connection between the battery ignition switch and starter motor circuit may be defective. Check the spark plugs and distributor head. Often, only the plugs will have to be replaced; always carry spares.

2. If the engine stops with grinding and clanking noises, serious damage is probably at hand. If no noise occurs, an electrical fault is probable and should be traced as above. If it hesitates and stops, the fault is most likely with the fuel system. Check as per instruction manual. The fuel tank may be empty. If not, there is probably a blockage in the line, or the fuel pump may have malfunctioned. Blow out the fuel line. If still no result, dismantle or replace the pump.

3. Overheating will be caused by a blocked water inlet, a broken water pump, low oil level or a fouled propeller. In any case, if the temperature rises, turn off the engine immediately.

4. Drop in oil pressure. Stop engine and check oil level. Refill as necessary. Do not run engine unless absolutely necessary.

5. Uneven running is probably due to a fouled plug or bad timing. Replace plug. If unevenness persists, have mechanic check out.

See note 2

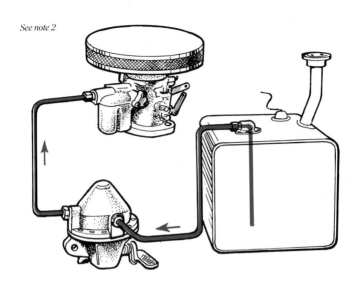

FIRE: Engine

• Shut off ignition immediately! Close fuel valve immediately!

• If engine room is equipped with self-activating extinguishing system, stand by with an appropriate hand-operated unit. Valves have been known to corrode at sea.

• If engine room is equipped with Halon extinguishing unit, close exhaust valve as soon as possible (even before shutting off ignition), as Halon can be sucked out through the engine before it can work effectively.

• If no automatic unit is installed, shut off ignition *and* fuel valve, open companionway steps or engine housing, standing well clear in case of burst of flame. Aim extinguisher toward fire and release, holding it as steady as possible.

1. It is vital to stop both fuel supply and ignition as soon as possible. This is especially true of gasoline/petrol engines, as explosion can occur both within the engine and back to the fuel tanks which, since they are usually located beneath or alongside the cockpit, can cause serious injury or death.

2. Please, please inspect and, if necessary, replace all engine room extinguisher valves at least twice each season. Since engine spaces are usually the most ignored places aboard —at least on sailing vessels—they are subject to all the ills of bad boat husbandry: oil accumulation, severe damp, grit and old rags. Valves cannot only be corroded, they can be blocked by grease and debris. Likewise, all wiring for all systems should be kept clear of the bilges, not run near or over working or hot parts of the engine, secured carefully and have all terminal fittings lightly coated with waterproof grease. If any of these precautions are ignored, very likely the system will fail when you most need it.

3. Using hand-operated extinguishers is not difficult, but does demand calm and intelligence. Everyone on board should be thoroughly acquainted with their operation, and you should have fired one off in practice, with crew present. The important thing is to hold them steady, pointed directly at the source of the flame. If necessary, brace yourself against a bulkhead or counter.

4. Engines are, of course, rarely out in the open. They are covered by hatches, companion steps or casings. If you are in the cockpit when the fire commences, get below before you open the engine compartment. You will not be able to direct your firefighting from above and unless there is a readily removeable engine hatch in the cockpit sole, don't try! Actually, cockpit engine hatches probably should not be opened, as the flames shooting out will be sure to burn someone.

5. If the fire gets out of control while you are below, DO NOT ATTEMPT TO ESCAPE THROUGH THE COMPANIONWAY! Use the forward hatch, and prepare to abandon ship.

6. In the event of *any* fire, have the

See note 3

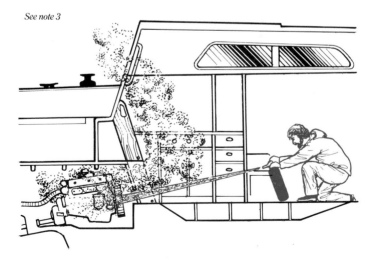

crew prepare the life raft or dinghy to stand by. Unless you are aboard a steel or aluminum boat, the chances of a runaway blaze not causing the boat to founder are minimal. Fiberglass, unless layed-up with fire-retardant resins, will soon turn into an inferno. If you cannot contain the fire, don't fight in vain. GET OFF THE BOAT!

See note 5

FIRE: Stove

- **Shut off fuel valves immediately!**
- **Alcohol and kerosene (meths and paraffin) fires: smother with fireproof blanket.**
- **Alcohol (meths) can be put out with water. However, water can also spread the fire.**
- **Solid fuel fires: use water or sand.**
- **Diesel: use dry powder or chemical fire extinguisher.**
- **Propane, butane, CNG: use extinguisher.**

See note 3

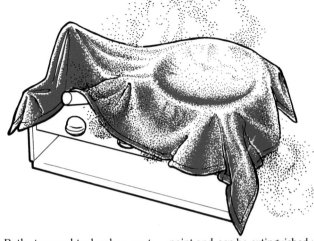

1. Both stove and tank valves must be closed. If stove valve cannot be reached because of flames, shut off tank valve and attempt to rip out hose. Some modern installations have remote control valves, either mechanical or electrical. These can be wired so as to simultaneously cut the fuel supply at both of the valve locations.

2. Alcohol, though rarely used except in the USA, has a low flash point and *can* be extinguished with water. However, the splashing water can also carry flaming alcohol with it, possibly igniting curtains, upholstery or even the container of spirits used for preheating the burners.

3. Fiberglass or other flame-retardant treated blankets can often successfully be used to smother flames. They must be close at hand.

4. Wood and coal fires can, of course, be put out with water. How-

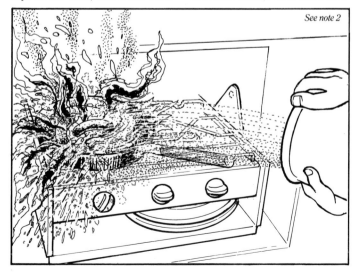

See note 2

ever, it may be handier to keep a container or bag of sand nearby. It will be safer—no steam—and usually

See note 5

OFF

See note 4

easier to clean up afterward. This applies to both heating and cooking stoves.

5. Propane and other gas fires are the most dangerous. Flames can travel these fuel lines much faster than with other fuels. A fail-safe device must be fitted to the stove, and every precaution must be made to keep all

equipment in prime operating condition. Explosion is the greatest risk. If a flare-up occurs, immediately shut off the gas and apply a fire extinguisher. Use the utmost caution when lighting a gas stove. Constantly check the system for gas leaks. With the exception of compressed natural gas (CNG) the entire class of fuels is heavier than air, and can be ignited by the simple act of striking a wrench against the engine block.

6. Keep the stove clean! A grease fire can cause just as much damage as any other. Either smother or use a fire extinguisher.

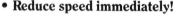

FOG

- **Reduce speed immediately!**
- **If on a compass course, adhere to that course.**
- **Sound appropriate signals.**
- **If position is known, consider using depth sounder for contour navigation.**
- **If radar is aboard, follow the appropriate measures.**
- **Post a lookout forward.**

1. Fog is usually accompanied by little or no wind. However, there are times and places where dense fog will coexist with strong breezes. In such situations, decrease throttle if under power or reduce sail more than you would normally. In dense fogs, visibility may be down to less than 100 meters, and anything other than dead slow ahead poses a real threat to the vessel and crew.

2. Human senses become less than reliable in foggy conditions: sounds are distorted, shapes appear and disappear, ships creep in and out of banks that suddenly close in. The only reliable navigational tool in such situations is the traditional ship's compass. Of course, you have made sure it is corrected and compensated before setting out. TRUST IT! No matter what your senses indicate, the compass is a safer bet. It is not subject to psychological pressures, it doesn't drink, and it won't fall overboard.

3. Fog signals: international rules:

> One blast: I am turning to starboard.
>
> Two blasts: I am turning to port.
>
> Three blasts: I am going astern.
>
> Five blasts: Beware! I am in doubt concerning your intentions.
>
> Short, long, short blasts: Warning!
>
> Danger of collision.

These are to be sounded on a horn or whistle. The ringing of a bell signifies a vessel aground or at anchor.

4. If attempting to home in on an audible signal, remember that fog can distort apparent sound direction. Proceed with utmost caution.

5. Always post the best-sighted person in the bows. He will be able to

See note 5

SUNSEEKER

give some warning of impending danger. Prearrange signals with the helmsman.

6. Contour navigation—following a sounding line on the chart—can be most useful in fog conditions. You *must* know your position, and must have an accurate, calibrated depth finder aboard, as well as an adjusted compass with deviation table. You then proceed to take soundings in a continuous run in the charted direction. Any deviation from the charted sounding line will become immediately apparent from the soundings.

One person should man the chart and depth sounder and call out bearings, course and soundings to the helmsman.

7. Radar is not often found aboard small yachts, but recent developments are putting it in the range of affordability, and scanner size and power requirements are decreasing. Radar takes practice, but if you have a set, you will no doubt have figured out how to use it. Depending on range, it can show you exactly what is ahead of you in most, if not all, conditions.

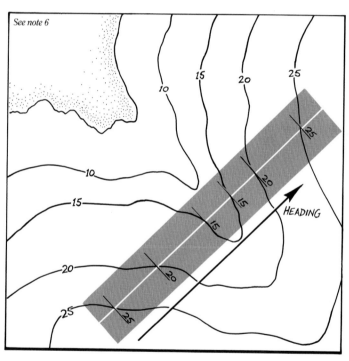

Rounding a headland in fog

Accurate DR approach, you find yourself in fog with a headland to round. Fig. 1, A is your DR plot. Give yourself a large area of uncertainty, say 8 percent instead of 5 percent of distance sailed, then take the two worst points on the circle: A_1 the most easterly and A_2 the most southerly. A, B, C would be your normal fine weather course, but if sailed from A_1 or A_2 would run you ashore. Fig. 2 shows a course 265°, 8 miles; 223°, 7.5 miles; 180° onward if sailed from A_1 or A_2 would take you clear of the headland.

Points to remember:

1. This course must be corrected for tidal direction prevailing at the time.

2. Your area of uncertainty is growing continually and if the fog does not lift you should keep off after rounding the headland.

3. At all times you will be plotting radio bearings, listening for fog signals, using your depth sounder. DO NOT CUT INSIDE your safe course unless you are certain it is safe to do so.

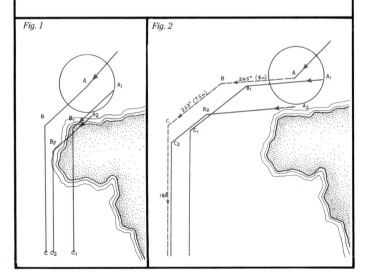

Fig. 1

Fig. 2

HEAVY WEATHER: Prepare

- **Assess sea state.**
- **Reduce sail or throttle back.**
- **Batten down.**
- **Secure crew.**
- **Decide on tactics (see below).**

1. When the weather deteriorates to a point where handling ship under reduced sail becomes difficult, when the size of the seas endangers the integrity of the ship, or when progress in a safe direction becomes near impossible, you are in danger. These three criteria are not the only ones, but they can serve as a good guide to the next set of maneuvers. All are dependent on weather fronts, winds and depressions (see WEATHER). The size and displacement of your vessel will have some bearing upon the meeting of the above conditions. Obviously a ketch of 15 meters LOA will be able to cope with large seas with greater assurance and safety than a power vessel of 10 meters LOA. Any sound vessel, however, can undertake precautionary maneuvers to allow more or less equitable coping with bad conditions.

2. When the wind pipes up, the first thing to do is to reduce sail. However, balance is equally important, especially when reaching or beating to windward. The larger vessel will be able to hold a course longer in a rising wind than a small boat, due to displacement, sail-carrying ability and a larger crew. A power boat, without the ballast or lateral plane of a sailing yacht, will have different

See note 2

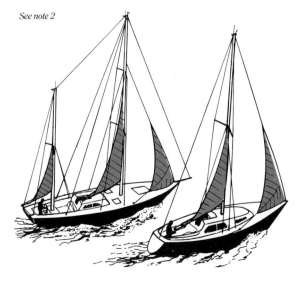

problems to cope with. The key is to keep green water from coming aboard. Running in a powerboat demands keeping speed at one with the wave length, plowing to windward invariably demands throttling back, whilst progress in beam seas is very much a function of the dynamic stability of the hull. When the weather is truly nasty, an appropriate reduction of speed is invariably the best seamanlike judgment.

3. Everything on deck and below must be secured in heavy weather. Sails, anchors, lines, life raft, crew must be attached to the boat in a manner that precludes loss overboard. Crew especially should be in life harnesses. Anchors should be given double lashings with heavy line…a loose object of such shape and weight can easily hole a hull given the opportunity. Below decks, batteries have to be tied down,

locker doors strong and secure—no friction or magnetic catches—books fiddled or lashed in place, stove gimbals closed, etc. Even floorboards should be able to be fastened, perhaps with button catches. In a knockdown, you will have a mess below, but any heavy object or glass or sharp implement can cause major injuries or even death. Try to avoid the worst. At the beginning of the season, it's even a good idea to tighten the engine bed fastenings. There have been cases of engines tearing loose from their mountings and causing boats to founder. Be sure to secure all hatches, ventilators, hatchboards and seacocks.

4. Much of what has been said above applies to the crew. Safety harnesses are *de rigeur* at night and in anything over a Force 5. They ought to be to government standard and constructed with two lanyards with

See note 3

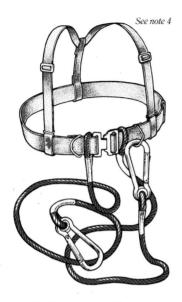
See note 4

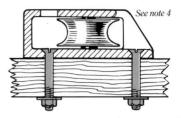
See note 4

proofed hooks/snaps. The deck attachment points must be through-bolted. Lacking such, or in emergencies, crew can lash themselves to binnacle or tracks.

5. How you will actually handle the boat in heavy weather depends to a great extent on the size of the ship, the capacity of the crew and the size of the seas and strength of the wind. Proximity to land plays a major role in deciding tactics. In a storm, with a lee shore in sight, the inability to beat to windward and an inexperienced crew, anchoring—providing the proper ground tackle is aboard —may be the only alternative. But every situation demands informed judgment—see the next section.

 # HEAVY WEATHER: Tactics

- **Helmsmanship.**
- **Sailing to windward.**
- **Reaching.**
- **Running.**
- **Lying ahull, heaving to.**
- **Survival conditions.**

1. The key man as the weather deteriorates is the helmsman. He (or she) needs to be fresh, alert, sensitive. He must keep a watch to windward for approaching waves, and must be a-ert to the need for sudden maneuvers. Keep him as protected, warm and dry as possible. When changing the guard, allow the relief to acclimatize himself to the course, conditions and "feel" of the helm before switching. A less experienced hand may require that sail be reduced to give greater control. This is a decision the skipper must make giving due regard to approaching fronts,

See note 2

need to reach port, etc.

2. Sailing to windward demands not only a good eye. The necessity of pacing the boat to the height of the waves is vital. The helm should luff slightly as he comes down the face of a wave, slowing the boat and allowing the bows to rise to the oncoming crest. Otherwise there is a good chance of burying the bows and causing loss and damage to the deck gear and crew. The boat should have minimum steerage when approaching the crest of the next wave, as the speed generated surfing down the back of the wave will usually be suf-ficient to ascend the next one. The maneuver is one of weaving, increasing and decreasing speed offwind and upwind so as to keep the boat moving with a reasonable motion and as little threat to ship and crew as possible.

3. In really heavy weather, sailing in a beam sea can be courting disaster. Cresting waves can fill cockpits, cause knockdowns, or stove in a deckhouse. In less momentous seas, a tendency to broach or a difficulty in steering will probably be experienced. Either shorten sail or head off with the wind on the quarter.

See note 3

See note 4

4. Running can be an exhilarating experience. However, when seas build to a point where steering becomes difficult, extreme care will be needed at the helm to avoid a broach. In gale or storm conditions, don't play racer and try to carry spinnakers. Rather, reduce sail to a point where the boat is moving at optimum speed, neither in danger of surfing so fast as to be falling off the wave tops nor so slow as to lose steerage way. In mid-ocean monster storms, the need will almost always be to slow the boat down.

5. To reduce speed in severe running conditions, several methods are available. With most modern sailing vessels, the sea anchor is to be avoided. The strains it puts on the ship are greater than the advantages, and there is usually not enough forefoot to the vessel for it to keep the bows to the wind. Trailing warps does work. However, they

demand a very slow-moving or still vessel. It may be most effective when lying ahull or heaving to.

6. Lying ahull is when all sail is stowed, tiller is lashed, and the ship left to look after herself. This can be a perfectly sound tactic, providing the sea room exists for leeward drift and some forward motion due to the area presented by rigging, spars and hull and tophamper. Some experiences have suggested that a shallow-hulled craft will be safer at this maneuver than a deep-draft one, as the deep keel can cause a tripping effect in certain sized seas, possibly causing a knockdown or rollover. It is also a good tactic for the single-hander in a small boat.

7. Heaving to is perhaps the simplest method of slowing a boat down and giving the crew rest in heavy going. The only maneuver required is

See note 5

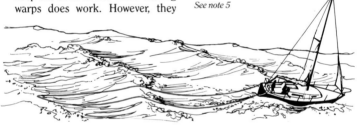

must be many and attached so as to distribute the strains around the ship. Occassionally, anchors can be trailed from warps or bundles of chain. However, be sure to rig tripping devices or you may never get the goods aboard again. Ideally, you will let them out as needed. This does assume, however, that several hundred meters of heavy line are aboard. Oil spread overboard either from the toilet or by means of a can or bag can be effective, but very few modern yachts ever have the capacity or availability of product effectively to deploy this method of calming the seas. Also, such tactics

to tack, leaving the headsail as is. Ease the main and lash the tiller to leeward. Then, depending upon adjustments of mainsheet and tiller, the boat will forereach slowly—dependant to some degree upon tophamper, sail area, keel depth, etc. The headsail should be brought in tightly before heaving to, and in heavier conditions, the main might well be dropped and secured. Of course, leeway will be made, and heaving to should not be attempted on a lee shore unless for a short time and with little sail and a deep-draft hull. Even then, adjustments must be made to allow for as little leeway as

See note 5

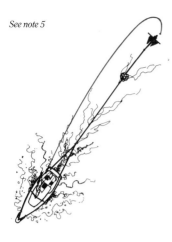

possible, perhaps by trimming the main to allow stronger forereaching. Chafe is always a problem when hove to; the practice is better with a working jib or storm jib than with a genoa or lapper. In very heavy going, some chafe protection around the sheet where it crosses the shrouds will not be amiss. The old saw about heaving to on the starboard tack has little relevance today, as most commercial shipping will not alter course, even if they see you. A controversial point, to say the least.

8. In "survival conditions"—Force 10 and upward—the only possible point of sail will be running. In fact, due to the strength of the wind and the severity and height of the seas, you will run no matter what. In such circumstances, it is best to rid the decks of any and all impedimenta that may be carried away or hamper such working of the deck as is possible. As mentioned before, oil or trailing warps is probably the best tactic. The warps should be streamed one at a time until the speed of the ship is lowered to the point where control is possible and following seas present the least threat. Extraordinary concentration at the helm is necessary and watches may be only one hour. If the lines trailed are in a bight and long enough to coincide with the seas aft, the bight may well serve to inhibit crests and smooth the attacking demons. In any storm or "ultimate" seas, stay with the boat unless

See note 6

See note 7

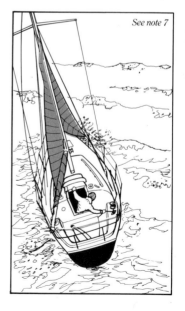

it is truly foundering. Life rafts, as shown by the Fastnet disaster in 1979, are too easily flipped, drift away or cannot be entered with any degree of safety. Even with improvements—ballast pockets, drogues, heavy tether lines—chances are that you will be safer in the mother ship so long as she remains tight. Whatever, be prepared!

See note 8

HOLING

- **Do not panic!**
- **Locate the hole immediately.**
- **Seal the opening with materials at hand (see below).**
- **If far from port, consider permanent repairs.**

1. If you strike an object, immediately go below and check for damage. If a hole has been rent in the hull near the waterline, sail on the tack to keep the hole above water. More than likely, the hole will be hidden behind bunks or lockers or beneath immoveable floorboards. There is only one solution: TEAR THE FURNITURE OUT! It hurts, but failure to do so immediately will result in probable foundering. Using a pry bar or axe or large spanner, wrench the offending woodwork (or glasswork) away.

2. Use either an umbrella patch or cushions stuffed into or against the hole to stop the major flow. Another interesting possibility is to use a plumber's helper over the hole, preferably from the outside. If the hole is well below the waterline, the inflow of water will be close to twice as fast as higher up, and may be much harder to reach. The storm jib, with lines at each corner, can be passed around the hull from the outside to from a patch. Reduce the speed of the vessel to allow the sail to stay in position. Weight one corner to allow it to sink below the water with chain or odd fitments shackled together.

3. No matter how hard and fast you work, a lot of water will enter the ship. The average bilge pump—25 gallons per minute—will be next to useless when up against a flow of over 200 gallons per minute, which is what you can expect from a hole about 4 inches in diameter. Only a high-capacity engine-driven pump can handle a flow like that, and then only if the engine has not been flooded. A bucket brigade can be of help, but the key is speed in locating the hole and speed and efficiency in stemming the flow.

4. Once the flow is stopped, or slowed to a leak, more permanent repairs can be effected. Perhaps the best material, in anything but a wood boat, is underwater-hardening epoxy paste. Follow directions, but do try to apply on the outside first with some sort of temporary board or backing held in place. Then apply to the interior. Remember to spread the paste well past the area of the hole to allow for good surface adhesion. In a wooden ship, boards and caulking can be used to first seal the opening from within, with further repairs made from the outside as conditions allow.

ICING

- **Slow the ship down.**
- **If conditions permit, run downwind.**
- **Prepare to send a man aloft with tools.**
- **If possible, reduce sail and power.**

See note 3

1. Ice will increase the topside weight, reducing stability and the righting moment of any ship. Slowing the vessel will permit gentler motion and more time to remedy the condition.

2. Since a sailing vessel is generally more stable when running, there will be less chance of capsize and an easier motion to work aloft. Keep up only enough sail to reduce rolling.

3. The only way to remove ice from the rigging is to hack it off with a mallet or the dull side of a small axe. Other than the deck man handling the bosun's chair, no one else should be on deck, as falling ice can inflict serious injury.

4. If conditions permit, keep up only a patch of sail to reduce rolling and power until the ice has been removed. Under any icing conditions, seek refuge as soon as possible. Not only is the ship in danger, but the crew can suffer from hypothermia and frostbite.

JURY RIGS: Masts

- **Assess the damage.**
- **Make an inventory of available parts, broken and otherwise.**
- **Design the new rig.**
- **Assemble the parts on deck.**
- **Raise the jury rig.**
- **Set sail.**

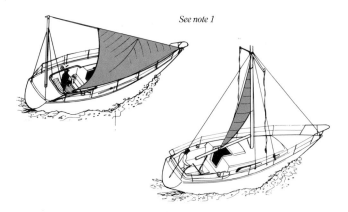

See note 1

1. Depending upon the damage inflicted to the mast (see DISMASTING), a jury rig may be an addition to what remains standing, or it may be an entire make-do structure. If the mast has broken above the spreaders, the storm trysail may work as a mainsail with only a forestay and backstay pieced together from spare wire and wire rope clips. If only the mizzen remains, a forestay can be fashioned—albeit at a very low angle —and a jib can be modified to be set flying from said stay. As long as the remaining bit of mast has retained the lower shrouds, a low-efficiency sailing rig is not only possible but relatively simple to fabricate.

2. If the mast breaks at or near deck level, a different set of criteria apply. First see what is salvageable from the leavings of your once noble spar. It may be possible to save stays, hardware or a section of the spar itself. Before you decide what you will do, see what you have to work with.

3. Having made an inventory of working materials—not forgetting oars, spinnaker and jockey poles, bunk fronts, etc.—sit below with a clean sheet of paper, some basic measurements (base of fore triangle, length of longest usable mast section, length of various salvaged wire, etc.) and a pencil and see what *might* be possible—what L. Francis Herreshoff called "thought experiments." It will be much easier than trying different combinations on deck in a seaway at night with the wind at Force 6. Perhaps the most important thing to remember is that the rig you design must be able to be created, hoisted and used by the available manpower and the available skills. If you are within sight of land, turn on the engine! However, if you are mid-ocean you will want to devise something that will take you where you want to go on the available rations and water aboard in whatever weather you may reasonably expect to have.

4. Having decided on the solution,

gather the crew, explain the jury rig to them and delegate one crew member to each task needed to raise the rig. Collect and assemble all the necessary parts. Do as much as possible with the new rig *on deck*. The less needed to do aloft, the safer. Make sure, for example, that all the "masthead" fittings are secured, that the correct length wires and ropes are tied off. You don't want to have to lower the whole mess if you can avoid it.

5. Depending on size and weight, raising the rig can be a job for one with a winch and a tripod arrangement or it can take the muscles of 10 strong men. Obviously, you wish to

See note 5

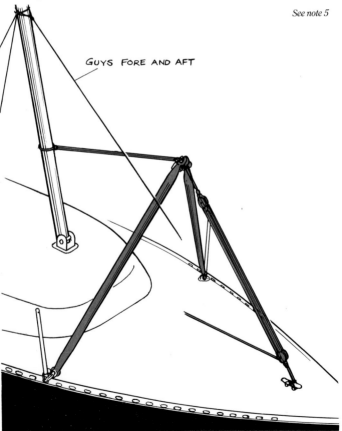

GUYS FORE AND AFT

get the thing up with minimal effort. The illustrations give some possible solutions.

6. Setting sail may mean adopting some odd and backended configurations. Jibs may be turned on end, or sewn together. Storm sails may be the best driving sails for a reduced rig, and setting them flying may be the best, and safest, means of propulsion. What is most important is to devise a sail combination that will get you where you wish to go. Quite often sprit sails, lateen rigs, makeshift schooners and squaresails will serve the purpose quite well if you know anything about them. Unfortunately, the modern sailor has little use for working sails of the past. The illustrations demonstrate their uses.

See note 6

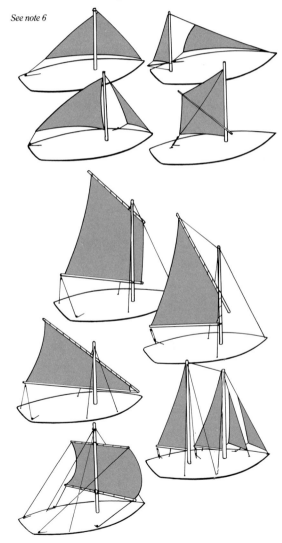

JURY RIGS: Rudders

- **Determine how the rudder is damaged.**
- **If only tiller, see BROKEN TILLER.**
- **If steering gear is unrepairable, see below.**
- **Repairs are different for outboard and inboard rudders.**

1. If the rudder is inboard and the stock has been bent, ignore it. Instead, you will have to fashion a rudder or sweep to work off the transom. If the blade is damaged, it may still be possible to steer the boat, albeit with reduced sail. However, if the response is minimal and you are still some distance from port, some sort of jury-rigged rudder will have to be constructed.

2. Should the steering gear be damaged beyond repair, an emergency tiller should be aboard. Since many more yachts are wheel-steered now than even 20 years ago, essential spares should be carried—cable, clamps, sprocket wheels, gears, etc. Obviously, you will never be covered for all contingencies. And, sooner or later, you will have to rig that emergency tiller. Accidents do happen which will incapacitate both wheel and rudder. Jury rudder again.

3. The simplest repairs are to a transom-hung rudder, which can be shipped and patched, or even replaced from parts fashioned from floorboards, hatchboards, etc. If the pintles and gudgeons are not bent or broken, repairs should be fairly straightforward, and if the rudder is wood can be accomodated with screws and bolts. If the rudder is fiberglass, the same methods can be used but reinforcement will be necessary in the form of load-spreading

washers (of metal or wood) and lashings. However, if the major portion of the blade has been torn away, and the fastenings between rudder and hull are left without integrity, a new rudder assembly will have to be fashioned.

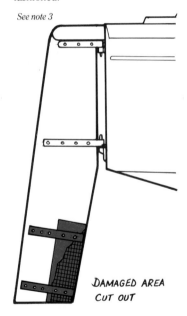

See note 3

DAMAGED AREA
CUT OUT

4. Inboard rudders pose a different set of problems. If the rudder bearing has been broken, and the rudder is slamming back and forth, potential exists for major hull damage or rupture, especially in a seaway.

Some means of locking the rudder in position, or even of shipping the entire assembly, will have to be devised. One good precaution is to drill a small hole in the trailing edge of the blade, with the foreknowledge that this will be used—should an emergency occur—to lead lines outboard and to the cockpit for steering. If the blade can be set, a rudder aft will still have to be fashioned.

5. Some self-steering wind vanes can be adapted to act as an auxiliary rudder. This potential might well be investigated when contemplating the purchase of a vane.

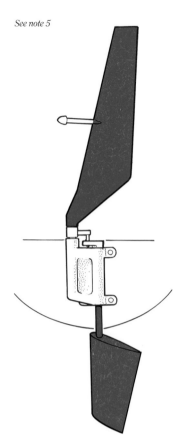

See note 5

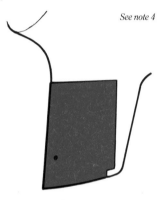

See note 4

6. To actually construct a new rudder, first gather the necessary materials: a pole—boom, spinnaker pole, oar (if long enough); a blade substitute such as a hatchboard or section of floorboard; line, lashings, bolts, tools needed, etc. Fasten the pole to the blade with through bolts, U bolts, or anything which will produce a rigid structure. Next, determine how to attach the assembly to the stern. As long as the blade will be deeply immersed, any method will do. However, stern shape will determine the most appropriate way of accomplishing this.

7. Perhaps the easiest stern to mount your new rudder will be virtu-

ally plumb, utilizing the pushpit horizontals as fastening points, with stout lashings to hold the two together. Reverse-counter transoms will demand a more deck-level approach with some fitting being used to hold the lashing. Traditional forward-sloping counters will best use the pushpit as above. Lacking guard rails aft, deck-level lashings will have to be used, remembering that with a single-point lashing some means will have to be devised to hold the blade in the water. Ballasting is one possibility. Another is to run lines from a hole in the *forward* edge of the blade near the bottom, outboard and forward to strong points on

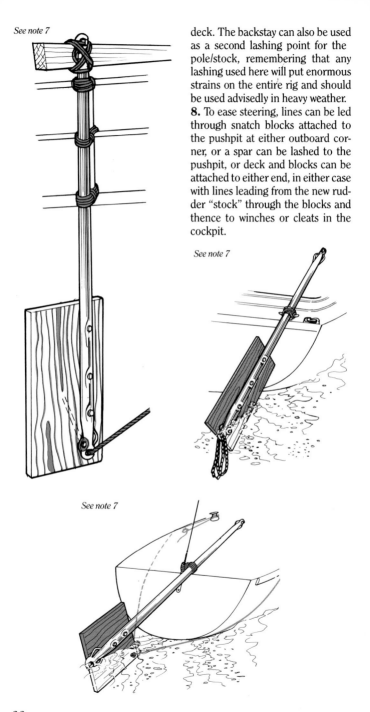

See note 7

deck. The backstay can also be used as a second lashing point for the pole/stock, remembering that any lashing used here will put enormous strains on the entire rig and should be used advisedly in heavy weather.

8. To ease steering, lines can be led through snatch blocks attached to the pushpit at either outboard corner, or a spar can be lashed to the pushpit, or deck and blocks can be attached to either end, in either case with lines leading from the new rudder "stock" through the blocks and thence to winches or cleats in the cockpit.

See note 7

See note 7

See note 8

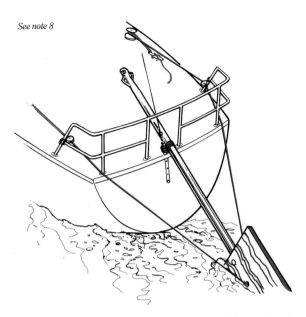

9. Despite advice to the contrary, it is always better to attempt to fix the tiller at the centerline. Even without a pushpit, some makeshift arrangement can be worked out on the afterdeck, usually by lashing a spar to the mooring cleats at the quarters and affixing the rudder stock to the spar. **10.** A drogue can be utilized for steering—tire, bucket or proper drogue—with steering lines attached to the drogue line with rolling hitches. To give the needed steering leverage, the ends of the

See note 10

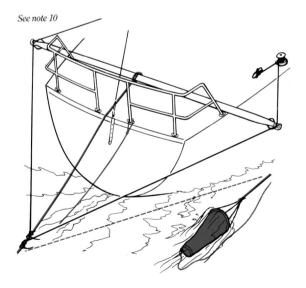

steering lines should be led through blocks on either end of a fairly long spar lashed to the stern. Be sure to rig a tripping line for the drogue.

You will find recovery difficult otherwise. Also, this arrangement, although the easiest to rig, will not offer the control of a jury rudder.

LEAKS

- **Locate the leak.**
- **If possible, isolate.**
- **Repair.**

1. Locating a leak may be much more difficult than you might imagine. Likely spots are seacocks, rudder gland, stuffing box, keelbolts, hull-to-deck join, deck fittings—in fact anywhere the hull or deck has been drilled, cut or opened to receive a fitting. In addition, tanks… water, waste or fuel. Too often, the leak is far from the spot at which water, etc. collects. You may have to trace the course.

2. A deck leak may be uncomfortable, but a hull leak, fitting or otherwise (skegs and keel sumps can crack from wracking strains in heavy seas) can be downright dangerous. Though the pumps may be able to cope, track it down. And don't forget the obvious: head intake hoses are

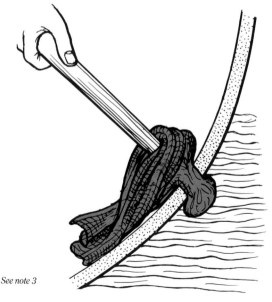

See note 3

68

usually not looped high enough. At rest this may be unnoticeable, but underway, especially when heeled, the head can overflow and cause a boat to founder. If the boat has sealed-off compartments, or if an area can be sealed off by makeshift means, do so until repairs can be safely effected.

3. Attempt to stop the leak with rags, caulking cotton, foam or neoprene or plugs. (Incidentally, all through hulls, even those with seacocks, should have a tapered softwood plug of appropriate size tied to the fitting with a lanyard.) Rubber and silicon caulking will NOT hold to wet surfaces. Underwater epoxy will, and should be kept aboard for such emergencies.

See note 3

LEE SHORES

- **Lay out a second anchor in the dinghy.** (See Fig. 1)
- **Hoist sails and let them run free.**
- **Carry the second anchor aft and secure it to a stern cleat.** (See Fig. 2)
- **Bring up the stern warp so that the boat is beam-on the wind.** (See Fig. 3)
- **Raise the bow anchor.**
- **Buoy the stern warp and let go.** (See Fig. 4)
- **Sail out to windward.**

1. Under most conditions a lee shore should be avoided only because of the possibility of heavy weather. If no choice exists, try to anchor as far out as is possible with safety.

2. If the engine is powerful, motor sailing should be attempted before trying to leave under sail alone.

3. In truly horrendous conditions, boats have survived by sailing in a half-circle and dropping as many anchors as are on board. Under these conditions it will not be possible to set anything from the dinghy and no other choice will exist.

4. Careful planning and coordination from all the crew will be necessary for these maneuvers to work. It

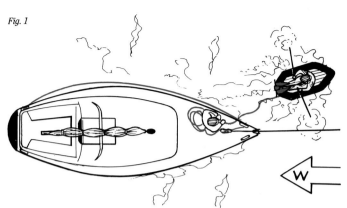

Fig. 1

will be difficult to keep the headsail from flogging itself to death and the jib sheets from fouling. However, your safety depends on this, and a crew member should be stationed at what will be the leeward winch to haul in as soon as the anchor line has been released. Another must be stationed at the mainsheet, leaving the helmsman free to concentrate.

5. When alone or shorthanded, it may be an advantage to sail the yacht out under only one sail—whichever is most efficient—keeping the decks relatively clear. If you must lose an anchor, do so...it costs less than the ship.

Fig. 2

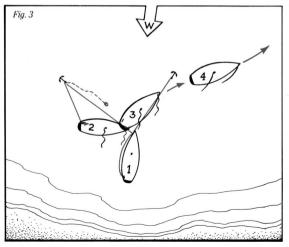

Fig. 3

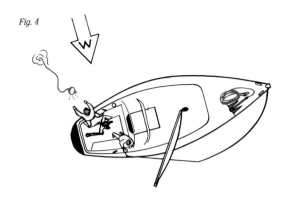

Fig. 4

LIFE RAFTS

• **Keep on deck.**
• **Use a fastening system that allows quick release, either patent or proper lashings.**
• **Keep serviced.**
• **Instruct the crew in proper usage.**
• **Tie the painter to a strongpoint on deck.**
• **Inflate by giving the painter a sharp jerk.**
• **Do NOT cut painter until all are aboard the raft.**

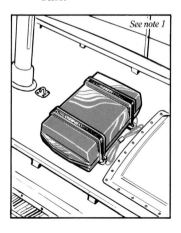

See note 1

1. It should be obvious that a life raft must be kept on deck or in a special raft locker. Nevertheless, many yachtsmen place it in a cockpit or lazarette locker where accumulations of gear and debris block access to it. Under-the-sole lockers are not recommended; too many people will be in the cockpit to make for easy access. Best location is either lashed to the coachroof fore or aft or the mast, or on the afterdeck or beneath the helmsman seat. Some newer boats have special recesses within the transom; these are fine if, in practice, you can get to them without en-

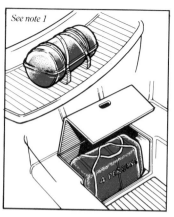

See note 1

dangering the crew. Best to keep all safety gear inboard if possible.

2. Don't use lashings that end up like the Gordian knot. They must be slashable with one stroke of a knife, or with a single tug on a line—some variant of a slippery hitch, for example. The lashings are best done up in natural cordage, as synthetics will slip too much. Manila or hemp—if you can find it—are good. Patent hold-down systems can be acceptable, providing they are constantly checked for corrosion or chafe. Like anything mechanical they are liable

See note 2

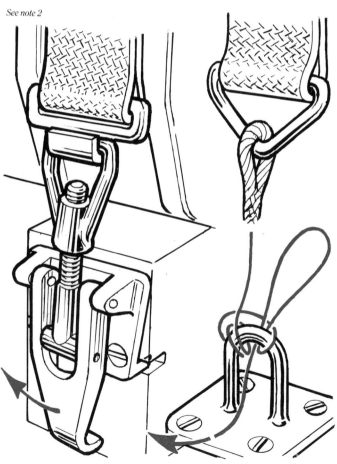

to seizure and breakdown when most needed.

3. Servicing is vital to life raft performance. Kept on deck, the raft, even in a fiberglass cannister, is subject to moisture penetration, fabric deterioration and valve failure. Yearly servicing by an authorized service center is vital. Yes, it is expensive. Yes, you need to do it. While we are on the subject, do buy a cannister raft. Valises are too subject to kicks, seepage and puncture. They should be avoided at all costs, no matter how well-protected you believe the raft to be. Also, pay a few dollars or pounds more and get a raft that is up to SOLAS standards. The difference, especially offshore, is worth it both in terms of construction and materials specifications and in terms of equipment.

4. The crew, every member of it, must be given proper instruction in abandon-ship and life-raft drill. Don't wait until it is too late. This is not to suggest you should inflate the raft to practice, but do use the dinghy to get the crew used to boarding a raft in rough seas and in a state of mock panic, something best done at one's moorings. Show them how to undo lashings, how to toss the raft overboard and how to inflate it. Make sure, when underway, that each crew member is supplied with a sharp—and properly protected—knife.

5. Depending where the raft is located, the painter should be tied to a deck fitting which is *through-bolted*. The strains upon raft and painter in rough seas when thrown are great. Stanchion bases, mast step, coachroof rails, pushpit are all appropriate choices.

6. NEVER ATTEMPT TO INFLATE THE RAFT WHILE IT IS ON BOARD! What with rigging, deck gear, trampling crew, wheel or tiller, etc., you will never be able to

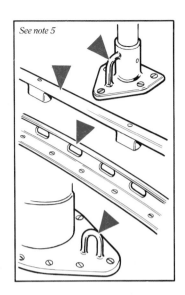

See note 5

See note 7

get it into the water, and if you do, the chances are you will rip the fabric or tear off a fitting or two. Always throw it clear of the ship.

7. The painter can become tangled. First make sure it is clear, then tug firmly. The throw of the raft may start inflation, but it is always best to make sure by giving the painter the approved and appropriate pull. If the

73

raft does not inflate, or only partially fills, get one person to attempt to start pumping. Make sure that individual is secure in a safety harness.

8. Should abandonment of the mother vessel become imperative, make sure *all* members of the crew are aboard the raft before cutting the painter. Rafts drift—especially in the conditions likely to be at the time—at a remarkable rate. There is little or no chance that contact can be reestablished with the yacht. As tragic experience has unfortunately shown, all too often, in panic, some crew member cuts that figurative umbilical cord prematurely. Someone is sure to be the worse for it.

See note 7

See note 8

LIGHTNING

- **In an electrical storm, get crew below.**
- **Stay well away from any metal fittings.**
- **If conditions permit the ship to be anchored or hove to, do it.**

1. Lightning is always unpredictable. Though it will rarely strike a yacht, enough cases exist, especially along the American eastern seaboard, to take all possible precautions. Since lightning will follow the most direct path to the water, it is up to you to provide such a path to help it on its way.

2. Though copper wire #8 is generally recommended for a lightning ground, much better is to use copper tubing, flattened at the ends con-

necting the lightning rod at the masthead with a keel bolt. In a boat with an encapsulated keel, a grounding plate should be attached to the hull as low below the waterline as is feasible.

3. Since very few European boats are fitted with lightning protection, in a sudden storm a length of chain, shackled to the cap shroud and dangled overboard (make sure it is long enough to remain under water) will act as a satisfactory substitute. If

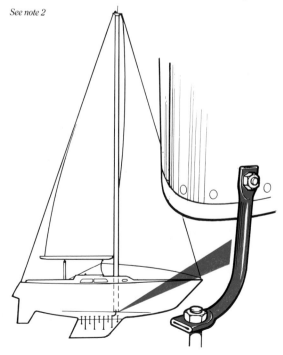

See note 2

time exists, tape the shackle end of the chain to the shroud to ensure positive contact.

4. Obviously, the helmsman remains in greater danger than the rest of the crew, especially if steering with a wheel. If possible, anchor; when at sea, heave to and join the rest of the crew below.

See note 3

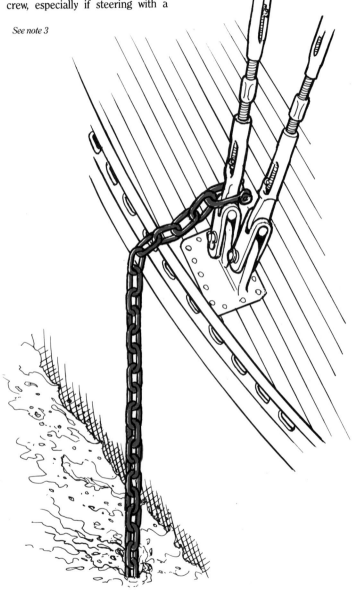

LIGHTS

- **Carry an oil- or battery-powered lantern.**
- **Never assume that proper lights will be shown.**
- **Be sure the lights are what they should be before hasty action**

See above

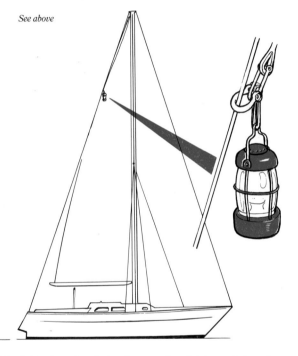

1. If the lights aboard go, hoist a lantern, preferably on the backstay. If hoisted to the spreaders, it will not be seen from leeward. See section on ELECTRICS.

2. Despite the International Rules, incorrect lights are often shown. Fishing boats are prime culprits, but yachts and merchants ships can also be offenders.

3. Always attempt to discern exactly what lights are being shown where on an approaching vessel before taking evasive action. Lifewise, even in approved anchorages, always hoist an anchor light.

4. Strobe lights, NOT in accordance with the International Rules, should be used only for distress and then only when necessary, as they can confuse a watch officer on the bridge of a large ship.

MAN OVERBOARD

- **Immediately throw a buoyancy device overboard, preferably with flagged pole and self-activating light.**
- **Have one crew member keep watch only on the man overboard, no matter what.**
- **If under sail, turn upwind.**
- **If under power, lower throttle.**
- **Commence pick-up procedures.**

1. All boats should have a life ring with man-overboard pole, flag, whistle, light and possibly a sea anchor attached. A horseshoe buoy will be easier for the person in the water to slip into. For the pole to be sighted, it must be at least 8 feet (2.5 m) long with a bright orange flag attached to the top. In heavy seas even this will be difficult to spot, and a longer pole is not a bad idea. Equally, the flag should be as large as is practicable to aid in sighting. A whistle will help locating the victim in any weather, while a light—preferably self-activating—will be a necessity in low-visibility conditions and at night. Sea anchors are often in bad repute, but a small cloth cone on a long bridle will certainly slow any drift and permit easier spotting and a more planned pick-up. No matter what the equipment, it should be mounted *outboard* of all rails, lifelines and deck encumbrances. Nothing can be worse than to attempt to release the gear and have it foul where it may be impossible to relese it. Ideally devices must be mounted on both sides of the cockpit at the stern within reach and ready-release by the helmsman. The pole can be fitted into a special release socket or

very lightly lashed to the backstay. *Very lightly* is important: the lashings must break only through the inertial pull of the life ring or horse-

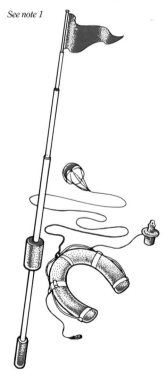

See note 1

shoe. Obviously, the idea is to have the entire kit in the water and as close to the man overboard as quickly as possible. Conditions exist where the shock of falling overboard will be enough to totally disorient and weaken the victim. It becomes absolutely necessary to get the floatation device to him or her and as near as possible quickly. In addition, the victim may have been hurt or possibly incapacitated in the fall. Finally, in heavy going and cold, survival chances are greatly lessened, and the less activity required of the person in the water, the less the heat loss and the chance of hypothermia.

2. As mentioned above, it is not easy to see someone in heavy seas. It is actually difficult to see a man overboard in almost any weather. The need for a crew member with good eyes and better powers of concentration is obvious. But for such a person to be truly effective, he must be left alone, not bothered, not expected to do anything but *keep an eye on the victim!* This cannot be too highly stressed. If the man in the water is lost sight of for but an instant, he may never again be spotted. Certainly, every sailor has practiced man overboard drills, but usually in gentle conditions and without panic or the sense of urgency required when a real living mass of flesh goes over the side. It's a lot different in reality.

3. Once the flotation materials are launched and a spotter is at work, then and only then should maneuvers to recover the person take place. Under sail, turn into the wind.

See note 4

This will allow the boat to keep way, yet slow her down by enough to prepare the crew for recovery measures. What you want to do is to get into a position to be able to pick up the man in the water from windward. (See following section on pick-up.)

4. Under power, there is less to do in working the boat, but perhaps greater potential danger to the victim. Under "slow ahead" describe a circle in the water so that you approach the person in the water from behind and to windward. When you are in drifting reach or just alongside (the forward third of the hull), STOP THE PROPELLERS FROM TURNING. Obviously, you can throw the gears into neutral. In calm weather, shut off the engine if you are in clear water. The danger from the propellers is frightening, and cases are on record of persons being dismembered or killed by a fast-turning prop. On a power boat, the freeboard, even aft (except on a fishing boat) will be appreciably higher than aboard a similar-length sailing vessel. If a stern door or swim platform is available, the person can best be hauled up from there. However, getting a soaked body up a meter or more of slick topsides is a maneuver that demands some forethought.

 # MAN OVERBOARD: Pick-Up

- **Get to windward of man overboard.**
- **Come about.**
- **Leave foresail backed.**
- **Let mainsheet fly.**
- **Secure helm to leeward.**
- **As boat drifts slowly toward person in water, prepare to get him or her on board.**

1. What you are doing in the above steps is *heaving to*. It allows the abandonment of actual sailing work, and the best apportionment of crew for retrieving the person in the water. Boat speed can be easily corrected by using the main or repositioning the rudder for angle of drift.

2. Depending on what course you are at the time of the accident, different maneuvers are more or less appropriate for successful positioning of the boat. See the diagrams.

3. If you cannot see the person overboard and conditions are good, sail or motor a reciprocal course. If the weater is foul or shows signs of deteriorating, begin a search from upwind of the approximate position you lost your crew. Keep records of time and distance sailed, and take into account current, tides and wind speed—all of which will affect the drift of the person in the water to a much greater degree than the ship. The search may be carried out to windward, on a reach or running. In each case you will have to tack back and forth, running parallel lines over the search area. See the diagrams.

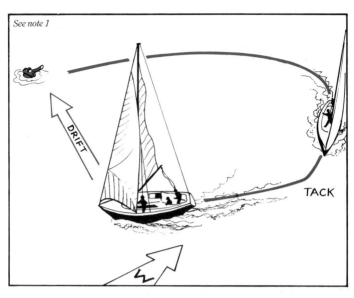

See note 1

DRIFT

TACK

W

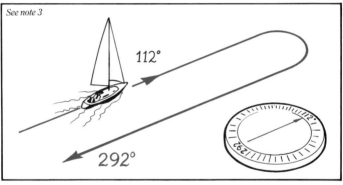

See note 3

112°

292°

See note 3

TIME 1735
DISTANCE SAILED ¾ M
CURRENT . WESTERLY
WIND SPEED 15 knts
DIRECTION SSE
TIDE 35 M to high

81

See notes 4 & 5

4. Once you have him spotted, and the boat under control, you must be prepared to get him into the boat. An average man, in foul weather gear and several layers of clothing, will add as much as 50 pounds (23.5 kilos) to his dry weight with immersion. This is not inconsiderable, and must be taken into account in any maneuver to get him back on board. NOTE: THE MAN IN THE WATER SHOULD PRACTICE A FEW PRECAUTIONARY MEASURES TO PROLONG HIS STRENGTH AND CHANCES OF SURVIVAL. HE MUST KEEP HIS CLOTHING ON TO CONSERVE BODY HEAT. HE MUST NOT SCREAM OR ATTEMPT TO SWIM TOWARD THE BOAT. IT WILL ONLY CONFUSE THE CREW AND DEPLETE HIS STRENGTH RESOURCES. HE SHOULD UTILIZE THE GEAR THROWN TO HIM IF POSSIBLE AND WAIT, USING ONLY THE WHISTLE ONLY WHEN THE MOTHER SHIP IS IN SIGHT. ABOVE ALL, *DO NOT PANIC*!

5. To get the survivor on board, several methods are possible. If he is injured or exhausted, lower a sail with all corners secured by lines to the ship. If he can do some of the work himself, a bosun's chair or bight of rope can be lowered to swing around his arms, allowing him to sit in it and be winched aboard. If a platform or boarding ladder is permanently attached to the stern, have him grab a bight of rope and maneuver him to the stern with a crew member on each quarter to assist boarding. In boats with transom-mounted rudders, a set of steps can be installed on the rudder blade from below the water line to allow easier boarding. DO NOT ATTEMPT TO HAUL A VICTIM ABOARD BY HIS ARMS!

6. Single-handed sailors have the most to worry about in man-overboard situations. You must always trail a poly (floating) line with a buoy attached to the end of it. This should be about 25 meters long. If you are sailing under self-steering gear, some means of disengaging the gear is necessary. One possibility is suggested in the illustration. A permanently mounted ladder with a lanyard attached to release the lower

See note 6

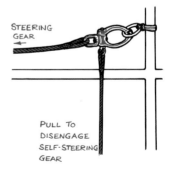

STEERING GEAR

PULL TO DISENGAGE SELF-STEERING GEAR

half, or the transom steps mentioned above, should be included in fitting out the boat. In power boats, the trailing line must be bridled to avoid fouling the propeller and might be rigged either to shift the gears into neutral or shut down the ignition when given a sharp jerk.

MAST CLIMBING

- A halyard has fouled, a tang fractured, etc.
- Reduce boat speed and head off on a reach.
- Rig bosun's chair on spare halyard.
- Have crew member stationed at winch.
- Rig downhaul and safety line.
- Crank up.

1. First ascertain if there is a way to free the line or ignore the damage without going up. If you are near port, you may be able to jury-rig an arrangement to get you in without trying to work in a seaway at the masthead. Remember, the pitching moment is much greater high up, especially if 75 kilos of mass is suddenly hanging on for dear life. Most repair jobs at the top are two-handed affairs, and for effective work both body and legs must be secured and braced. If any possible way exists to carry on without clambering up, take it, *unless the crew or ship will be endangered through failure to take action.*

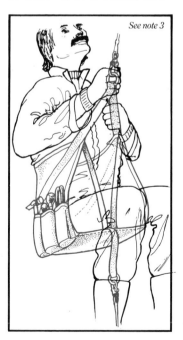

See note 3

2. Tearing along at hull speed will in no way aid the crew who must be at the masthead, either once there or climbing. Lower the boat speed as much as possible while maintaining steering way. A reach will steady the boat and, depending upon the tack, can actually provide a more secure position at mast top. Sail may have to be reduced.

3. The traditional bosun's chair is both uncomfortable and potentially dangerous. The wood seat can slam into the mast, causing more damage. The newer, all-cloth models with restraining straps and tool pockets can be both safer and allow for more efficient and quicker work. The crew who has volunteered to go up must be *totally* secured before ascending. A downhaul must be rigged to the chair, and a line with snap hook or some other expedient means of wrapping around the mast to keep the occupant in position should be affixed, preferably around the person, not just to the seat. A safety harness can be employed, providing that the tether is not too long. All the tools that might be needed should be secured by lanyards if possible. In fact, it is a good idea to keep basic tools permanently ensconced with the bosun's chair: vise grips, screwdriver, marlinspike, adjustable wrench/spanner, etc. The assumption of rigging the chair on a spare halyard demands some forethought. Spinnaker halyards may be too light to be safe, the main halyard may be jammed, and the jib needed to maintain forward motion. In such a situation, it may be wise to use the spinnaker halyard as a messenger to carry a heavier line through its masthead sheave. In a fractionally rigged boat, a spare main halyard might well be permanently rigged.

4. Hauling the man aloft demands a strong wincher, enough turns (at least four) around the winch and a good braking turn around a cleat. The point is to get someone up safely, not fast. A second crew member on the deck should handle the

See note 4

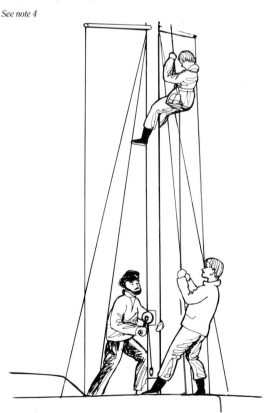

downhaul, keeping it taut and making sure that swing is kept to a minimum. If the main is down, the safety line should be used by the man aloft, breaking it only at the spreaders.

5. Frankly, the precautions mentioned above should be adhered to in *all* weathers. At night, a flashlight/torch should be carried aloft, possibly taped to the upper arm with gaffer's tape. Gloves are another recommendation, but they must be full-fingered and leather. Anything else will either chafe or slip. Deck boots will protect the legs and a foam-filled life vest will help absorb bumps while not overly hindering the wearer's movements.

6. If for some reason the bosun's chair is not usable or one isn't on board, a substitute will have to be devised. Lots of possibilities exist, of course, but whatever is used must be of irreproachable integrity: a bowline on a bight or an emergency boarding ladder. Do *not* use a fender unless it is the type that allows the line to run through it; standard inflatable fenders are not reliable enough in their grommeting to hold a man's weight under stress conditions. And, should you use one of the other alternatives, remember to pad it well. Raw wood or rope can cause serious injury aloft in high winds and rolling conditions. The poor sucker at the masthead has enough to worry about!

7. There will be times when no halyard is available for hauling a bosun's chair. A rope or plastic ladder,

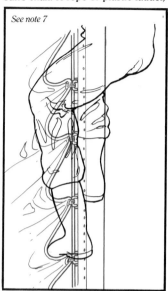

See note 7

or a wood and rope ladder, can be used but demands much vigilance and agility as well as a messenger line to haul it up: it's usually far too much bother and too time-consuming when you need it. The main can be slacked slightly (only in fairly large boats) and used as a ladder. However, the slides *must* be metal. Plastic slugs can fracture, causing a rapid descent of catastrophic speed and force. Remember to follow the safety precautions!

MEDICAL EMERGENCIES

- **Do you need to save a life?**
- **Do you need prevent the situation from getting worse?**
- **Must you relieve pain and suffering?**
- **Do you need outside assistance?**

1. The above questions are not meant to solve any specific problem, but they must be asked in any situation concerning injury or sickness. Though most accidents aboard will be minor—cuts, seasickness, sunburn, colds and flu—many others will require more than two aspirin and a cup of tea. You must be prepared to cope with anything short of major surgery, especially if you intend a transoceanic passage of any length. To this degree, every yacht should be equipped with an up-to-date and constantly renewed first-aid kit, including appropriate medications for the areas to which you plan to voyage. Also aboard must be a modern first-aid manual *that has been read by at least two crew*. Any member of the crew who has a specific chronic ailment, drug allergy or medication requirement should inform the captain of such *before* setting sail. It is up to the captain to assess the situation and make any decision of the crew's suitability based on the remoteness of the landfall, the conditions likely to be encountered and the general physical condition of the crew member.

2. If the person has stopped breathing or has no discernable heartbeat you must act immediately to save that person's life. Bleeding will kill a person much less quickly—unless it is a major hemorrhage of a major artery—than lack of oxygen or no heartbeat.

3. If the person is not subject to any immediate threat, you must decide if the condition might worsen. Many injuries and illnesses can get more serious, but the most common might include: burns; infections; exposure; poisoning; concussion; fractures; unconsciousness; open wounds; chest pain. If you decide that the person is in no immediate danger, continue to port. Otherwise, consult your medical guide.

4. The greatest concurrent problem with any injury at sea may be fear. Not only take appropriate action, but reassure the injured person. Care, concern and will can play as important a part as anything to help alleviate distress and aid someone on the path to recovery.

5. Can you cope? Certain medical conditions will be beyond your ability to treat. If you are far from shore, you must use your judgement and common sense, and do everything in your power to aid the patient with what you have at hand. Certain infections can be held at bay with antibotics. Certain fractures can be immobilized until a doctor is at hand. But other conditions may be impossible to do much about. Internal hemorrhaging, heart attack, certain types of poisoning, extreme hypothermia may be beyond you.

Following are some general guidelines for treatment and diagnosis. They should be used in conjunction with a reliable medical first-aid manual. They are not infallible, and any responsibility is in the hands of the person administering the first aid.

Abdominal pain: This can be mild or severe. Until the cause is clear:
> Put the patient to rest.
> Allow neither food nor liquids.
> Do not give laxatives.
> Give pain medication if required.

If pain is persistent, vomiting frequent, diarrhea severe, abdomen firm and tender, seek medical assistance. Very severe pain accompanied by very hard, tender abdomen can indicate ruptured appendix, ulcer or ovarian cyst. Infection is possible and antibiotics every six hours should be considered until professional advice is secured.

Antibiotics do *not* cure everything! They are useless against viral or fungal infections. Follow doctor's recommendations closely as to dosage and types to carry aboard. Duration of treatment should be no more than a week to 10 days. Cautions:
> Avoid sunlight.
> Never give to pregnant women or children under eight without specific medical advice.
> Allergic reactions or lack of response should indicate need for immediate medical consultation.

Bleeding: Use sterile, soft, absorbent material and apply pressure. Small cuts will usually stop bleeding after a short while; larger cuts should have the material taped over until further action can be taken. Cleanse with soap and water or hydrogen peroxide. Only use a tourniquet in extreme, heavy bleeding emergencies.

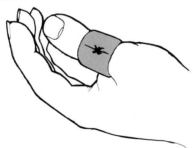

Burns: For all burns, the immediate treatment is to apply cold water liberally. Use soaked cloths, either fresh or salt. Avoid running water and ointments, creams or sprays. With anything more than a first-degree burn, cover with sterile petroleum jelly, gauze and a sterile dressing. For second- and third-degree burns seek immediate medical attention. Life-threatening burns can cause shock and the danger of infection. Give oral fluids, keep dressings in place, give pain killers and antibiotics if more than 24 hours will elapse before a doctor can care for the patient.

Cardiopulmonary arrest: Heart attack or lung malfunction. Follow these steps:

Determine consciousness.

Open the airway, tilt back the head with neck lifted.

Give mouth-to-mouth resucitation; if after four breaths the chest doesn't move, attempt Heimlich maneuver.

Feel for pulse, if there but no breathing start mouth-to-mouth at one breath per five seconds.

If no pulse, start CPR (see below).

CPR: Your local Red Cross offers training in this lifesaving technique. If you haven't taken the course, follow the steps below only if the situation is genuinely desperate:

Place victim on hard surface.

Place the heel of the hand over the sternum about 2 inches from the lower tip.

Place other hand at right angles on top of the first and press down hard enough to depress the breastplate an inch or two. Release. Pause. Repeat.

Give victims 2 breaths after each 10 to 15 depressions. This is about the correct rate.

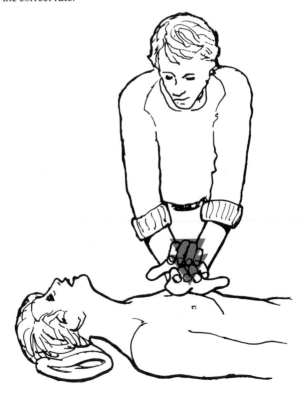

Choking: Use the Heimlich maneuver:

Deliver back thumps with a closed fist between the shoulder blades. With hands clasped around the victim, make abdominal thrusts between the breastplate and the navel—4 thumps, 4 thrusts. Continue until choking is relieved.

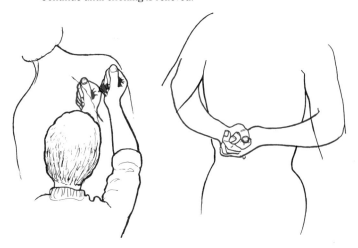

Cold: Wear loose-fitting warm clothes; keep hands, feet and head covered. Get out of wet clothes as soon as possible. Drink and eat warm substances. Do NOT drink alcohol. *Frostbite:* Warm affected part in 40 to 42 degree Centigrade water rapidly. Pain medication may be needed. Seek medical assistance. If unavailable, warm soaks twice a day, clean dressings and separation of toes and fingers will prevent tissue deterioration.

Constipation: Eat lots of fruits, vegetables and roughage. Colace are usually effective and convenient to take. Avoid laxatives. A glycerine suppository or a warm-water enema may be best with prolonged constipation.

Cuts: Use strip or butterfly bandages to close the cut, apply pressure and keep it clean. Larger cuts will require stitching and prompt medical attention. If signs of infection appear, use antibiotics.

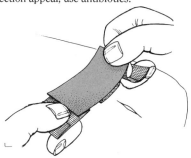

Diarrhea: Keep up fluid intake; most patent medicines will make the patient feel better but will not *cure* the cause. Pepto-Bismol may be the best, according to a recent study. If the diarrhea is accompanied by high fever or bloody stools, use ampicillin as per directions. Seek medical care as soon as possible as complications are possible.

Eyes: For eye irritations, glare, foreign bodies, wash with fresh water, cover with loose-fitting bandages. Seek medical care if pain or visual impairment persists. Always wear sunglasses.

Fever: Use aspirin or acetaminophen, no more than 10 grains every 4 hours. Do NOT increase dosage. Cool sponge baths can aid in reducing fever. Dress the person lightly unless suffering chills. If fever is high and persists, infection is possible and antibiotics are called for. If no change after 48 hours, seek immediate medical attention.

Fractures: Immobilize immediately. Apply ice packs if possible. Give pain medication. Do NOT try to set the fracture, merely keep it from moving with splints or bandages. Keep tight enough but not so tight as to stop or hinder circulation. Seek medical aid immediately. Compound fractures—where skin has been broken—will require cleansing of the wound and antibiotics.

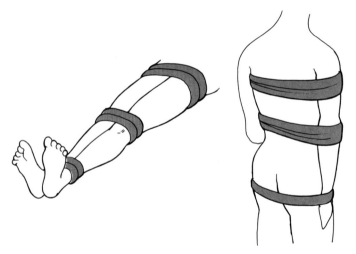

Heat: Keep protected, even on cool days. Drink what you need to feel comfortable. Do NOT ration water. The body can store water and the old saw about rationing has been fairly convincingly disproved by recent U.S. Army Survival School studies. If heatstroke occurs, intensive, rapid cooling is called for. Put victim in cold-water bath (plugged cockpit) or wrap in soaked sheets. Sea water works well. After body temperature has dropped to 102° (40.6°C), cease cold treatment. Massage arms and legs to promote cooling circulation. As soon as possible start feeding cool liquids by mouth. Follow-up medical care is necessary as potentially serious damage can be inflicted on internal organs.

Pain: Pain is a symptom. Specific medication will not cure the cause unless the cause is known. For relief: aspirin, acetaminophen. For medium pain, codeine, Darvon, Percodan, Talwin; these all require prescriptions. Ask your doctor for specifics. Severe and persistent pain: morphine or Demerol. These are dangerous drugs and should be avoided for all but the transoceanic passagemaker. Ask for specifics from your doctor.

Poisoning: Internal: cause vomiting as soon as possible, except for petroleum products; after vomiting stops give milk, mineral oil or bread to absorb the poison and keep it from absorption into the system. Skin contact: wash thoroughly with water, remove clothing. Breathing: get into fresh air immediately. So many poisons exist it is well to contact a doctor by radio as soon as you are able to. He may be able to help. If victim is comatose, get to land immediately, even if it means calling for air rescue.

Respiratory infections: The infection cures itself. Flu, colds, sore throat, bronchitis are best treated with rest, lots of fluids, aspirin, decongestants, etc. In cases where fever develops or persists and no improvement is seen, antibiotics may be called for. They should be kept up for 10 days, even after symptoms have disappeared.

Seasickness: The most effective medication I know is Bucladin. This is a prescription drug better known in the UK than in the US. Some changes have occured in the composition over the years. According to *The Yachtsman's Guide to First Aid Afloat*, by Earl Rubell, M.D., the correct formula should be:

Buclizine HC1	50/0 mg
Pyridoxine HC1	10/0 mg
Scopolamine HBr	0/2 mg
Atropine S0$_4$	0/05 mg
Hyoscamine SO$_4$	0/05 mg

Patent medicines work or don't work according to the individual. Chronic seasickness must be dealt with as best one can. Milder forms can often be cured by focusing on a distant horizon, keeping blood sugar levels up, and avoiding interiors or exaggerated sense of motion.

Shock: You can help prevent shock by keeping the victim warm, dry, reassured, and breathing regularly. If the victim goes into shock, there is little that can be done without transfusion and medical facilities.

Urinary infections: Non-specific: drink lots of fluids; Pyridium can be administered to relieve burning and frequency of urination. Wait a week before administering anything else. If infection persists, administer Gantrisin or tetracycline. Seek medical advice.

Specific (venereal): gonorrhea symptoms—discharge, burning urination—are treated with antibiotics and medical follow-up. Syphilis can be diagnosed as a painless ulcer at the point of sexual contact. Seek medical advice immediately. Syphilis is a complicated disease and is beyond the scope of any first-aid treatment.

PROPELLER

- If prop fouls, turn off engine immediately.
- If near shore, anchor.
- If offshore, heave to.
- See DIVING.
- Cut impediment free.

See note 3

1. Failure to shut down engine could cause damage to the gearbox.

2. Since a crewmember will have to dive to clear the obstruction, follow the methods set out in the section on DIVING. Stopping the vessel will aid immeasureably.

3. It may help to raise the stern of the boat by concentrating weights forward. Also, a partially inflated dinghy can make a useful work area as well as cushioning the stern in any sort of swell.

4. It will probably be easier to saw rather than cut the rope turns on the prop. A hacksaw blade or keyhole saw will be found most effective and can be lashed to a makeshift wood handle.

See note 4

PUMPS: Bilge

- **If bilge pump clogs, disassemble at once, remove debris.**
- **If pump still will not function, check the diaphragm, replace if necessary.**
- **If draw is minimal, check the strum boxes (strainers) at termination of hoses.**
- **If handle breaks, use short section of pole, cut to fit female pump handle receptacle.**
- **Navy-type pumps may need total disassembly.**

1. Most modern bilge pumps are of the diaphragm type. These will function in situations where older pumps would have long failed or clogged. However, even a pump which has a capacity of moving 30 gallons per minute (115 l) will not be very effective with a major hull breach. In such a case, only an engine-driven pump will suffice. And if the engine ceases to function, a bucket brigade will do far more than either.

2. Always carry spares for all pumps. A new diaphragm can be installed in

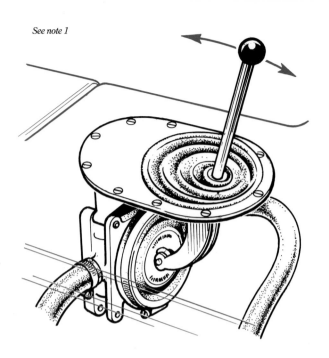

See note 1

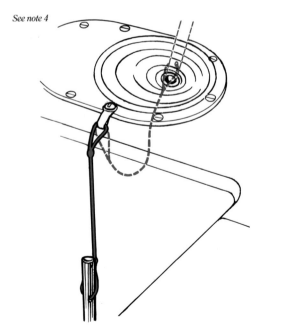

See note 4

approximately five minutes, providing access is reasonable. The same is true of strainers; you must be able to reach them.

3. Installation is vital to proper pump efficiency and safety. Too often, bilge pumps are mounted so that a cockpit locker lid must be opened to operate them. Mount cockpit pump with a through-deck fitting, properly capped and watertight and accessible to the helmsman. Any offshore boat should have a second pump operable from below.

Most stock boats are equipped with pumps of much too small capacity. Minimum should be 25 gallons per minute (95 l).

4. Pump handles will break. Either keep a factory spare, make sure the interior and exterior pumps have identical handles or carry a hardwood dowel of correct dimensions. Also, it is a good idea to drill a hole through the handle and tie it with a light lanyard to a spot where it is always at hand, near the pump. A spring clip will also work well.

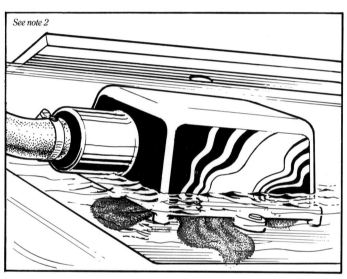

See note 2

RIGGING

- **If any part of the standing rigging fails, *immediately* remove or decrease strain upon that side of the rig.**
- **Tack, do not gybe.**
- **Jury-rig a replacement or repair.**

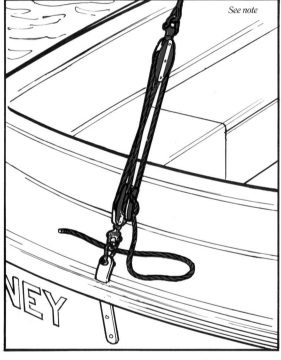

See note

1. Depending on conditions, you can continue sailing. However, if calm, and forestay fails, it's best to let well enough alone, rather than risk the chance of the mast falling aft into the cockpit. When things start getting rough, such luxuries will not be possible and getting the sails down and the rigging break mended will be most important. If the backstay breaks, lead a halyard aft and tension with a Spanish windlass or block and tackle—the vang, perhaps. You will head up during this process. If the forestay ruptures, head downwind, then use a spare halyard shackled to the stemhead for support. If the halyard is long enough, this can be led aft to a winch for greater tensioning.

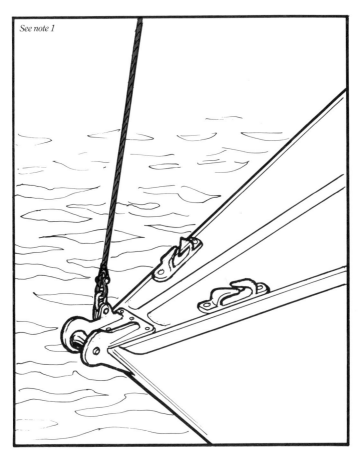

See note 1

2. Should a shroud go, immediately tack—gybing will place undue strain on the rig, and could carry it away—and head off so as to put the least strain on the failed part of the rig. Try to take sea state into account, as undue pitching and rolling can cause almost as much damage as the original fitting letting go.

3. Your most useful equipment for jury rigging, besides a spare halyard, will be wire rope or bulldog clips. These should be galvanized, not stainless steel, which has a tendency to slip. If a stay has fractured at the turnbuckle fitting end, form a bight or loop with the wire and use at least

two clips to form an eye, which may be lashed or shackled to the turnbuckle or attached directly to the chainplate with a block and tackle. If the stay has broken at the masthead, sooner or later someone will have to go aloft. If no spare length of wire is aboard, the eye should be made at the end of wire aloft (do this while still on deck), which can then be shackled to the masthead fitting or tang. The now shorter stay can be attached to the chainplate or turnbuckle with shackles and a length of chain. If the wire has broken midway, make two eyes and fasten them with shackles, lashings or chain.

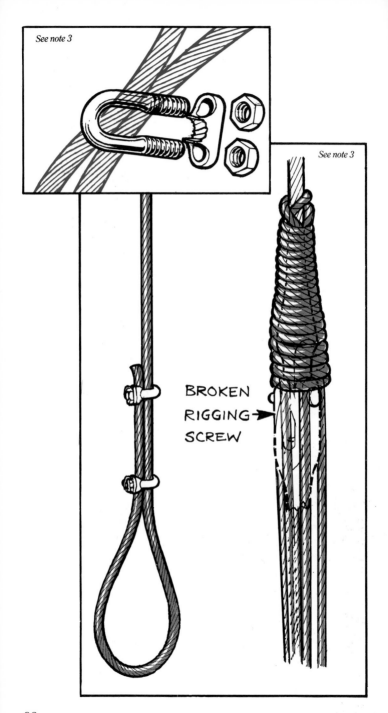

98

4. Rarely does it occur, but when a turnbuckle fractures or lets go, the solution is actually much simpler than when the shroud or stay breaks. Either replace it with another turnbuckle, use a lanyard or lash the stay in place. Times come, though, when the turnbuckle is frozen tight. This is the result of lax maintenance, and you should curse yourself soundly. Since you are presumably sailing on a tack that takes the strain off the fitting, remove the offender by slipping a clevis, lash the stay temporarily, and use two mole wrenches to break the freeze. Replace the turnbuckle.

5. Should wire need to be cut, use either wire cutters or a cold chisel. However, whip or tape the wire to either side of the proposed cut first to prevent unlaid strands or eye-damaging bits of flying steel. Wire rope is prone to a life of its own, and another crew member should hold it fast. Lacking the personnel, lash the wire with light stuff to keep it in place.

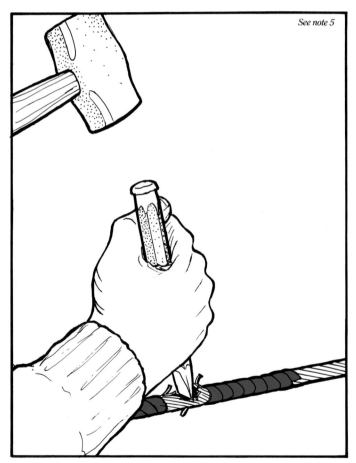

See note 5

SAIL REPAIR

- If main-sail tears along a seam, reef.
- If tear is in cloth, patch with tape on both sides.
- If slides rip off, lash.
- If boltrope tears, patch.
- If clew fitting fractures, lash.

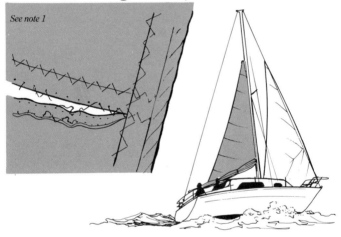

See note 1

1. Should the main rip along a seam, or should the stitching come undone, and the tear is below the reef points, reefing is the simplest immediate solution. If the tear is high up, lower the sail immediately, and continue to sail under foresail alone. Or hoist the storm trysail in its place until repairs can be effected. With roller reefing, there is greater latitude in just how large or small the reef can be, but after a certain point the main will lose any efficiency, driving power or ability to balance the foresail, and should be dropped and replaced.

2. Should the sailcloth, not a seam, tear, best patch it on BOTH sides, either with rigging tape or even better,

the special self-sticking sail-repair patches sold for the purpose. In calm conditions, patches of sailcloth and "instant" waterproof glue can effect a temporary repair. The best solution is to drop the sail, replace it with another and have the sail sent below for proper stitched repair.

3. A stitched sail repair requires, in synthetic cloths, fine needles—not the canvas-piercing monsters of old —Terylene/Dacron thread, and a comfortable sewing palm. Beeswax is not really necessary with modern materials. Double the thread, knot the two loose ends, and close the tears with a series of herringbone stitches. With synthetic cloth, anything from six to 10 stitches per

See note 4

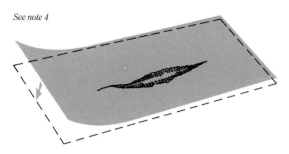

inch, depending upon the weight of cloth, thread, etc. should be adequate. If the tear is larger than your four fingers minus the thumb can enter, it should be patched. A patch can be done in several ways. Use approximately the same weight cloth as that of the sail. Use two layers—one on either side—of lighter cloth. Seal or fold under the edges. Tape the patch in place. Fasten using a seam stitch. Note: try to line up the weave of the sailcloth and the patch if possible. With very large rips this may not be achieveable with the materials at hand. Any patch is better than none.

4. Adhesive-backed sail-repair patches are sold for small jobs.

These will usually work for a while, but are neither permanent nor particularly suited for heavy weather. They can be temporarily used until you or your sailmaker makes a permanent repair.

5. Lost slides are all too common, especially with plastic and nylon. A few spares ought be carried, and can easily be sewn on or, if the sail has been grommeted along its luff, can be lashed with light synthetic twine or tape.

6. Boltropes are easily repaired with a patch around the rope on either side, extending several inches outward from the rope. Sew through on both sides, remembering to keep the patch around the rope as tight as

See note 5

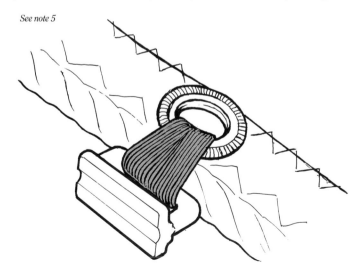

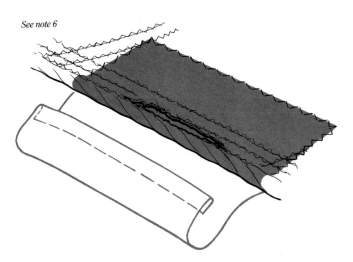

possible, increasing the diameter as little as possible and thus avoiding jams.

7. If the clew fitting goes by the board, a stout lashing will temporarily suffice. More permanently, sew in a new grommet, sew in a rope grommet, sew in a D-ring or O-ring replacement. In any case, make sure that the corner of the sail is heavily reinforced, and the stitching is doubled or quadrupled. All sewn repairs are similar: if overlap is possible, do it. If you can double stitching, do it. If both sides can be patched, do it.

See note 7

SALVAGE

- **Salvage is a subject fraught with dispute and complication.**
- **Make a contract beforehand if possible.**
- **Be prepared to handle later court action or arbitration.**

1. A salvor must establish certain proofs to make a claim:

The vessel was in peril.

He made a voluntary decision to aid the distressed vessel.

He risked his life and vessel to save the distressed vessel.

He achieved his aim and succeeded in aiding.

2. If a contract is agreed upon *before* rescue efforts commence, no further claims can be made. A verbal agreement with witnesses present is adequate, legal and binding.

3. No matter what, few claims are settled without court or arbitrator attentions. Be prepared for a long and complicated procedure. Seek legal advice, specialized if necessary. The procedures are not related to land law and can easily overwhelm an amateur.

4. Accepting tows or aid does NOT entitle the aiding party to claim salvage, nor claim ownership of property. Consult a qualified attorney or solicitor to determine the extent of claims or damages.

SIGNALS

- **Before sending out any signals make sure you really are in distress.**
- **Use the appropriate signal.**
- **Use the signal only if there is a fair chance it will be seen or heard.**
- **When using pyrotechnics, use caution.**

1. Far too often distress signals are sent for inappropriate reasons or for no reason at all. If the engine has died and you are merely becalmed, *no* reason exists to send any signal. Patience is the solution.

2. Don't use flares in the daytime and smoke signals at night. Don't use an EPIRB when five miles from port. Don't attempt using VHF distress channel in midocean. Common sense should dictate the signal most appropriate for any situation.

3. Equally a question of propriety, don't waste signals, especially pyrotechnics. Unless you are near land, or sight another ship, chances are your visual signal will not be seen. This is especially true of open water passages, a great many of which are away from shipping lanes.

4. Pyrotechnics, either hand-held or fired, must be used with caution. If any way exists to practice legally,

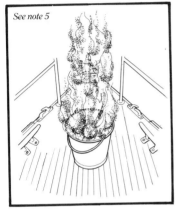

See note 5

avail yourself of it. When the time comes to use them, do so without panic. Potentially fatal accidents can and have occured. The chance of starting a fire exits. Always set off flares away from tanks, gas bottles, engines, etc.

5. In a pinch, a metal bucket of flaming rags, a gun fired, and most importantly a signal mirror can work. Obviously, the burning materials must be used with extreme caution, and are not advised aboard GRP boats. A signal mirror, even if torn from the head's bulkhead, can, providing the weather cooperates, be extremely effective. It is seen from the bridge of a large ship with greater ease than dye markers or other daytime visual signals.

6. IMPORTANT: all signals must be used with caution, calm and a regard for the realities of the seas. If you can—whatever the manner—get safely to port, do so on your own. The cost to others should be considered before haphazardly requesting assistance.

See note 5

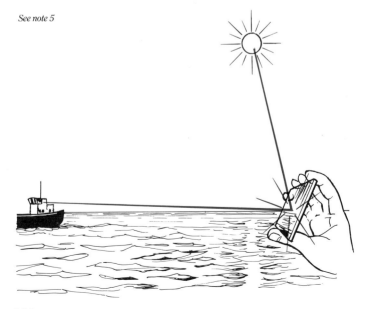

See note 4

TILLER: Breakage

• Outboard rudder: jam a section of boathook or an oar between the rudder cheeks and lash in place.
• Outboard rudder: if tiller fits to either side of rudder blade, lash poles or scrap wood around blade top.
• Inboard rudder: cheek-type fitting, as first suggestion above.
• Inboard rudder: socket fitting, opening may not be clearable. Use visegrip/molegrip pliers with lines led to coaming blocks and thence to winches.

1. Cheeks at rudder head may also be damaged. Scrap plywood can be used as reinforcement on either side, lashed temporarily. Later, when time permits, drill three staggered holes through ply and rudder cheeks and throughbolt. Makeshift tiller can still be lashed between the new cheeks or else drilled and then throughbolted, making for a stronger, more responsive jury tiller.

2. If nothing else is at hand, use two long fiddles, such as are often found to keep settee cushions in place. These are usually fastened with self-tapping screws and can easily be re-

fitted later; they make an elegant, either-side-of-the-rudder-head tiller.

3. Cheek fittings are usually bronze or stainless steel and the wood may have swelled between them, the tiller having broken slightly above the fitting. Knock out retaining bolt and swelled-wood fragments. This will require a chisel and mallet. The same tools can be used to shape the wood replacement. Remember, any jury tiller will be weaker and offer a less than ideal position for maximum leverage. Go easy.

4. Socket fittings are usually impossible to clear quickly. A possible solution is to use a section of whisker/jockey pole or any strong tubing *over* the socket fitting. Another possibility, if you can clear the socket, is to use a spare stanchion, chilly to touch but of unrivaled strength.

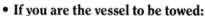

TOWING

- **If you are the vessel to be towed:**

  1. Drop sails and secure.

  2. Position one crew member at the helm.

  3. Secure bitter end of hawser to strong point on deck (see below).

  4. When towing boat approaches from leeward side, heave hawser to her waiting crew.

  5. Instruct towing vessel as to your maximum speed and allow her to proceed, stationing a crew member forward to pass signals.

- **If you are towing vessel:**

  1. Approach the vessel to be towed from her leeward side.

  2. When crossing her bows, either pass or accept towing hawser.

  3. Try to fasten the towline to strong points forward of the rudderpost to aid in maneuverability.

  4. Proceed ahead slowly, handing out the towline until taut.

  5. Position one crew member aft to see that line remains taut (to avoid fouling

**your propeller) and to accept hand signals
from the disabled boat.**

- **Towing under sail:**

  **1. Pass the disabled vessel's bows from
  leeward.**

  2. Heave towline as you pass her bows.

  3. Head off on a reach or run.

1. Dropping sail is obviously not ap-
plicable in a powerboat. However, if
there is a sea running, a very small
steadying sail aft may make steering
easier for the towed boat and maneuverability greater for the tow-
boat.

2. Crew should be positioned at the
helm, forward and at standby. All
must be ready for immediate action,
especially as might concern recovery
of the towline.

3. Many contemporary boats do not
have adequate foredeck cleats. A
towing hawser handed by a commercial vessel will be quite large, and
even if the cleats were enormous,
very likely they would only be
through-bolted to a backing pad.

Decks have been ripped up. The
ideal foredeck attachment point will
be a samson post properly locked
into the keel or stem. Lacking this, it
is perhaps best to secure the towline
around the base of the mast, or, on a
powerboat, around the entire house.
Alternatively, the towline can be attached to a bridle led either side of
the house to the cockpit winches
and then cleated. In any case, it is a
good idea to bend a piece of (com-
paratively) light stuff to the hawser
and tie its bitter end to a deck cleat;
the bend to the hawser should be
forward of the stemhead. In case the
towline slips or chafes through at the
stem, this "safety" line will make it
that much easier to retrieve it.

See note 3

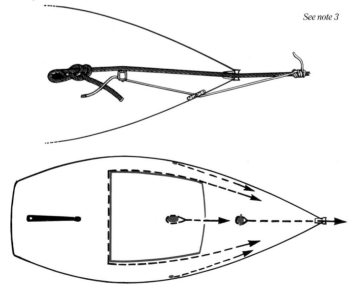

4. Always approach from the leeward side of the disabled vessel. You will then be able to avoid either drifting down on the vessel or overshooting it. Whether you should accept a towline or pass over your own is not a clear point of maritime law. (Read entry on SALVAGE.)

5. All tows must be undertaken at slow rates of speed. Quite often, commercial ship operators do not fully understand the limits that can be imposed safely upon a yacht under tow. What happens is either the towrope snaps or your foredeck has a good chance of disintegrating.

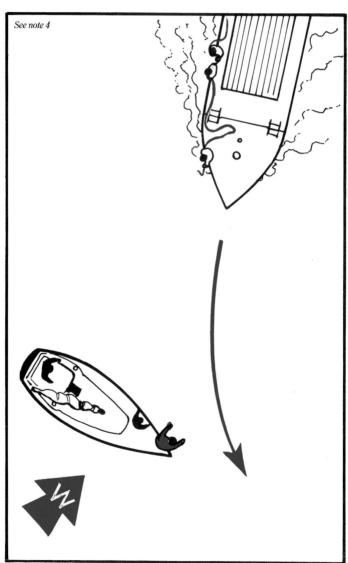

See note 4

See note 6

6. Hand signals are the only way to communicate properly during a tow. These must be arranged prior to the actual commencement of towing, and crew should be stationed on both vessels expressly for the purpose of signalling.

7. If you are the towing vessel, a bridle, carrying the towrope to either quarter or to the winches, will enable you to maintain a straighter tow and allow for more fluid handling, as well as keeping the rope clear of the propeller. It will prevent your vessel from skewing from side to side and will better distribute the towing strains.

8. Under sail, tows can be very efficient. They also allow for better communication between vessels,

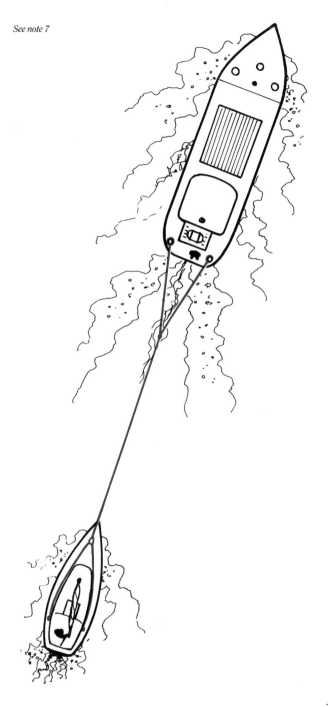

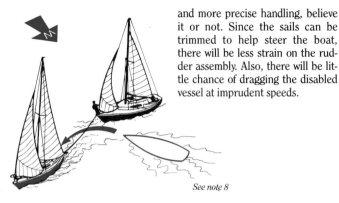

and more precise handling, believe it or not. Since the sails can be trimmed to help steer the boat, there will be less strain on the rudder assembly. Also, there will be little chance of dragging the disabled vessel at imprudent speeds.

See note 8

WATER

- **To obtain, use rainwater, distillation.**
- **To purify, use bleach or iodine.**

See note 1

1. Rainwater can be caught in awnings, buckets, from the mainsail, etc. Allow it to run for a few minutes to rinse off any salt adhering to the catchment. Distillation can be carried out using a large pot on the stove with a funnel-like cover secured over it. A tube should run up and over, then down to another container. Wrap the central portion of the tube with rags. As the water boils, pour cold seawater on the rags; this will condense the steam in the tube and leave the crystalized salt in the pot, produce reasonably salt-free water.

2. Household bleach can be used to purify and make palatable drinking wter that may be tainted or old. Use 2 drops per quart or litre of clear water, double if the water is cloudy. Iodine (2%) can be used instead in the ratio of 5 drops per quart or litre of clear water, double if the water is cloudy. Let stand for an hour before using and aerate by pouring back and forth between containers.

APPENDIX A

Spares and Tools

Following, courtesy of Jeff Neuberth, is a list, or rather three lists, of spare parts, tools and oddments that might well be carried aboard any boat, but especially offshore, when you have no one but yourself to undertake repairs.

▶ Boats Under 30 Feet ◀

TOOLS
8" adjustable wrench
medium-sized pliers
medium-blade screwdriver
10" vise grips
pocket rigging knife with spike
Dacron pouch or waterproof bag to carry tools

SAIL REPAIR KIT
scissors
sailmaker's wax
palm
seam ripper
hot knife
three spools waxed polyester
needles (5 each #s 15 and 17)
one roll Rip-stop tape
3'×3' piece of adhesive stickyback Dacron/Terylene
light thread for spinnaker repair, telltale yarn
nylon dittybag containing all of the above

SPARE PARTS
assorted stainless steel nuts, bolts, washers, sheet metal screws
bulbs for compass and running lights
winch pawls and springs
cam cleat springs
cotter pins (stainless steel, two of each size used and split rings)
small clear plastic tackle box to contain above

ODDS AND ENDS
one roll of silver duct tape
tube of clear silicone seal
one can penetrating lubricant
small can 3-in-1 Oil
felt-tip marker pen (black)
can Never-Seize
nylon dittybag to hold the above

▶ For Boats From 30 To 45 Feet ◀

TOOLS
Allen wrenches
chisels (one cold)
drills (hand drill plus set of bits)
files (8" mill bastard, one medium size rattail, one triangular)

hammer (medium ballpeen)
50' measuring tape
nail set
oil stone
pliers (channel locks, needle nose, 2 regular)

saw (hacksaw plus at least 10 high-
speed blades)
screwdrivers (6 assorted sized
regular, 2 Phillips head, 1
jeweler's set)
vise grips (7″ and 10″)
wire brush
wire cutters
work gloves
wrenches (8″ and 10″ adjustable,
set of combination—open end
and box)
wood tool box or dry organized
area to store all of the above

ELECTRICAL PARTS
spare bulb for each light aboard
three each spare fuses for each kind
aboard
assorted wire crimps
wire stripper/crimper
flashlight batteries and bulbs
continuity tester
black electrical tape

ENGINE AND MECHANICAL
SPARES
three cans of oil for hydraulics
hydraulic hose and assorted end
fittings
transmission fluid
set of engine filters
assorted grits wet/dry sandpaper
complete set engine belts
enough oil for oil change
new voltage regulator for each
alternator
6′×6′ canvas drop cloth with
grommets
piece of plywood
piece of wood (2×4)
assorted hose clamps
drift punch

SPARES
assorted nuts, bolts and washers
five of each size cotter key used
aboard
assorted clevis pins
assorted D shackles
assorted snap shackles
one standing rigging toggle
one genoa car
winch pawls
winch pawl springs
winch roller bearings

SAIL REPAIR KIT
scissors
sailmaker's wax
two palms
two seam rippers
hot knife
light thread for spinnaker repairs
six spools waxed polyester
needles (10 each #s 13, 15, 17, 19)
Rip-stop tape
3′×6′ piece of stickyback Dacron/
Terylene
yarn for telltales
25′ seizing wire
three D rings
sailmaker's pliers
nylon bag to hold all of the above

SEALERS AND LUBRICANTS
two-part epoxy
two tubes clear silicone seal
two cans penetrating lubricant
can 3-in-1 Oil
silicone spray
special grease mixture
rolls of colored tape
two rolls of duct tape
felt-tip marker pens (black)

▶For Yachts 45 Feet and Larger ◀

TOOLS
Allen wrenches (long and short)
awls (small and large)
block plane

chisels (one cold, two regular)
drills (brace, hand drill, 3/8″ chuck
variable-speed reversible electric
drill, two sets of metal bits)

files (8″, 10″, 12″ mill bastards, three wood files, two rattails, one triangular)

hammers (16 oz. ballpeen, baby sledge, claw and rubber mallet)

measuring gear (100′ measuring tape, fold-up ruler, calipers)

mirror (one retrieving)

nail sets (five assorted)

oil stone

pipe cutter

pipe length (for battering ram)

pliers (two channel locks, two needle nose, four regular in assorted sizes)

putty knives (two 1″)

saws (cross-cut, hacksaw and 40 blades, jigsaw and 12 blades)

screwdrivers (17 assorted regular, six assorted Phillips head, two off-set, one set of jewelers)

tap and die set (including 8-32, 10-24, 10-32, $1/4$-20, $5/16$-24, $3/8$-16, $3/8$-24)

tin snips

torch set

vise

vise grips (7″ and 10″)

wire brushes

wire cutters

work gloves

wrenches (6″, 8″, 10″ adjustables; 14″ pipe wrench, strap wrench, complete $3/8$″ drive socket set, complete set combination wrenches, popular-sized open-end wrenches)

utility knife and six blades

wooden tool box to contain the above

ELECTRICAL PARTS

compass light assembly

running light bulbs

spare bulb for each brand of light aboard

three of each kind of fuse aboard

assorted wire crimps

wire stripper-crimpers

flashlight batteries and bulbs

assorted sizes of wire

black electrical tape

silicone grease

multimeter

solder

soldering gun or iron

spare anemometer cups

spare wind vane

spare knotmeter transducers

tackle box for the above

SEALERS AND LUBRICANTS

two-part epoxy

two tubes clear silicone sealer

two cans penetrating lubricant

two non-aerosol cans 3-in-1 Oil

two cans silicone spray

special grease mixture

two rolls duct tape

two rolls of each colored tape

felt-tip marker pens (black)

Dacron bag to hold the above

SAIL REPAIR KIT

scissors

sailmaker's wax

two palms

two seam rippers

hot knife and spare tip

light thread for spinnaker repairs

eight spools waxed polyester

needles (one package each of #s 13, 15, 17, 19)

two rolls Rip-stop spinnaker repair tape

two 3′×6′ pieces stickyback Dacron

yarn (red, green and blue for telltales)

two weights seizing wire (25′ each)

three D or O rings

50′ tubular webbing

sailmaker's pliers

assorted weight sailcloth

roll 5 oz. Dacron/Terylene tape, 6″ width

spool $5/32$″ flag halyard

six awls

grommet set (stud, spur, mallet, die, rings, liners)

Dacron bag to hold the above

RIGGING PARTS
Nico-press tool (size of halyards, two preferable)
12 Nico-press sleeves for each size wire aboard
assorted stainless steel thimbles
assorted snap shackles
assorted D shackles
several lengths different weight wire (15″ each)
assorted rigging toggles
assorted clevis pins
assorted track cars
link plate set
spare main halyard
spare genoa halyard
good size turnbuckle
plastic fishing tackle box for above

ENGINE AND MECHANICAL SPARES
gallon of oil for hydraulic rigging adjusters
10′ length hydraulic hose, assorted fittings
two cans transmission fluid
oil for engine oil change
set engine filters, gaskets
complete set engine belts
voltage regulator for each alternator
6′ × 6′ canvas drop cloth with grommets
assorted hose clamps
piece of plywood
two pieces 3′ long 2 × 4s
drift punch
set of injectors

grease gun with special grease
two cans starting spray (Ether)
keel bolt wrench
rudder-packing wrench
spare set steering cables
master links (12) for steering chain and spinnaker pole chain

SPARES
clear plastic tackle box containing 12 of each size SS cotter pins
clear plastic box of nuts, bolts, and washers (12 each size including #s 6, 8, 12 and $1/4''$ $5/16''$, $3/8''$)
head repair kit: spare pump parts, diaphragms, impellers
hand pump for bilge, for changing oil
electric drill pump, hoses
sleeve bronze wool
12 sheets each wet/dry sandpaper in 220, 400, 600 grits
three sheets each crocus cloth, emery paper
spare packing for propeller and rudder glands

WINCH PARTS
12 pawls
24 pawl springs
assorted roller bearings
six split rings
toothbrush
tweezers
dental pick
extra handle
clear plastic box to hold the above

OPTIONAL
banding tool, bands, and clips

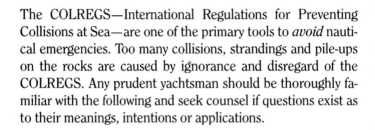

APPENDIX B

The COLREGS—International Regulations for Preventing Collisions at Sea—are one of the primary tools to *avoid* nautical emergencies. Too many collisions, strandings and pile-ups on the rocks are caused by ignorance and disregard of the COLREGS. Any prudent yachtsman should be thoroughly familiar with the following and seek counsel if questions exist as to their meanings, intentions or applications.

The International Regulations for Preventing Collisions at Sea

PART A.   GENERAL

RULE 1: *Application*

(a) These Rules shall apply to all vessels upon the high seas and in all waters connected therewith navigable by seagoing vessels.

(b) Nothing in these Rules shall interfere with the operation of special rules made by an appropriate authority for roadsteads, harbours, rivers, lakes or inland waterways connected with the high seas and navigable by seagoing vessels. Such special rules shall conform as closely as possible to these Rules.

(c) Nothing in these Rules shall interfere with the operation of any special rules made by the Government of any State with respect to additional station or signal lights or whistle signals for ships of war and vessels proceeding under convoy, or with respect to additional station or signal lights for fishing vessels engaged in fishing as a fleet. These additional station or signal lights or whistle signals shall, so far as possible, be such that they cannot be mistaken for any light or signal authorized elsewhere under these Rules.

(d) Traffic separation schemes may be adopted by the Organization for the purpose of these Rules.

(e) Whenever the Government concerned shall have determined that a vessel of special construction or purpose cannot comply fully with the provisions of any of these Rules with respect to the number, position, range or arc of visibility of lights or shapes, as well as to the disposition and characteristics of the vessel, such vessel shall comply with such other provisions in regard to the number, position, range or arc of visibility of lights or shapes, as well as to the disposition and characteristics of sound-signalling appliances, as her Government shall have determined to be the closest possible compliance with these Rules in respect to that vessel.

RULE 2: *Responsibility*
(a) Nothing in these Rules shall exonerate any vessel, or the owner, master or crew thereof, from the consequences of any neglect to comply with these Rules or of the neglect of any precaution which may be required by the ordinary practice of seamen, or by the special circumstances of the case.
(b) In construing and complying with these Rules due regard shall be had to all dangers of navigation and collision and to any special circumstances, including the limitations of the vessels involved, which may make a departure from these Rules necessary to avoid immediate danger.

RULE 3: *General definitions*
For the purpose of these rules, except where the context otherwise requires:
(a) The word "vessel" includes every description of water craft, including non-displacement craft and seaplanes, used or capable of being used as a means of transportation on water.
(b) The term "power-driven vessel" means any vessel propelled by machinery.
(c) The term "sailing vessel" means any vessel under sail provided that propelling machinery, if fitted, is not being used.
(d) The term "vessel engaged in fishing" means any vessel fishing with nets, lines, trawls or other fishing apparatus which restrict manoeuvrability, but does not include a vessel fishing with trolling lines or other fishing apparatus which do not restrict manoeuvrability.
(e) The word "seaplane" includes any aircraft designed to manoeuvre on the water.
(f) The term "vessel not under command" means a vessel which through some exceptional circumstance is unable to manoeuvre as required by these Rules and is therefore unable to keep out of the way of another vessel.
(g) The term "vessel restricted in her ability to manoeuvre" means a vessel which from the nature of her work is restricted in her ability to manoeuvre as required by these Rules and is therefore unable to keep out of the way of another vessel.
The following vessels shall be regarded as vessels restricted in their ability to manoeuvre:
     (i) a vessel engaged in laying, servicing or picking up a navigation mark, submarine cable or pipeline;
    (ii) a vessel engaged in dredging, surveying or underwater operations;
   (iii) a vessel engaged in replenishment or transferring persons, provisions or cargo while underway;
   (iv) a vessel engaged in the launching or recovery of aircraft;
    (v) a vessel engaged in minesweeping operations;
   (vi) a vessel engaged in a towing operation such as severely restricts the towing vessel and her tow in their ability to deviate from their course.
(h) The term "vessel constrained by her draught" means a power-driven vessel which because of her draught in relation to the available depth of water

is severely restricted in her ability to deviate from the course she is following.

(i) The word "underway" means that a vessel is not at anchor, or made fast to the shore, or aground.

(j) The words "length" and "breadth" of a vessel mean her length overall and greatest breadth.

(k) Vessels shall be deemed to be in sight of one another only when one can be observed visually from the other.

(l) The term "restricted visibility" means any condition in which visibility is restricted by fog, mist, falling snow, heavy rainstorms, sandstorms or any other similar causes.

PART B.   STEERING AND SAILING RULES

Section I.   Conduct of vessels in any condition of visibility

RULE 4: *Application*
Rules in this Section apply in any condition of visibility.

RULE 5: *Look-out*
Every vessel shall at all times maintain a proper look-out by sight and hearing as well as by all available means appropriate in the prevailing circumstances and conditions so as to make a full appraisal of the situation and of the risk of collision.

RULE 6: *Safe speed*
Every vessel shall at all times proceed at a safe speed so that she can take proper and effective action to avoid collision and be stopped within a distance appropriate to the prevailing circumstances and conditions.

In determining a safe speed the following factors shall be among those taken into account:

(a) By all vessels:
  (i) the state of visibility;
  (ii) the traffic density including concentrations of fishing vessels or any other vessels;
  (iii) the manoeuvrability of the vessel with special reference to stopping distance and turning ability in the prevailing conditions;
  (iv) at night the presence of background light such as from shore lights or from back scatter of her own lights;
  (v) the state of wind, sea and current, and the proximity of navigational hazards;
  (vi) the draught in relation to the available depth of water.
(b) Additionally, by vessels with operational radar:
  (i) the characteristics, efficiency and limitations of the radar equipment;
  (ii) any constraints imposed by the radar range scale in use;
  (iii) the effect on radar detection of the sea state, weather and other sources of interference;

(iv) the possibility that small vessels, ice and other floating objects may not be detected by radar at an adequate range;

(v) the number, location and movement of vessels detected by radar;

(vi) the more exact assessment of the visibility that may be possible when radar is used to determine the range of vessels or other objects in the vicinity.

RULE 7: *Risk of collision*

(a) Every vessel shall use all available means appropriate to the prevailing circumstances and conditions to determine if risk of collision exists. If there is any doubt such risk shall be deemed to exist.

(b) Proper use shall be made of radar equipment if fitted and operational, including long-range scanning to obtain early warning of risk of collision and radar plotting or equivalent systematic observation of detected objects.

(c) Assumptions shall not be made on the basis of scanty information, especially scanty radar information.

(d) In determining if risk of collision exists the following considerations shall be among those taken into account:

(i) such risk shall be deemed to exist if the compass bearing of an approaching vessel does not appreciably change;

(ii) such risk may sometimes exist even when an appreciable bearing change is evident, particularly when approaching a very large vessel or a tow or when approaching a vessel at close range.

RULE 8: *Action to avoid collision*

(a) Any action taken to avoid collision shall, if the circumstances of the case admit, be positive, made in ample time and with due regard to the observance of good seamanship.

(b) Any alteration of course and/or speed to avoid collision shall, if the circumstances of the case admit, be large enough to be readily apparent to another vessel observing visually or by radar; a succession of small alterations of course and/or speed should be avoided.

(c) If there is sufficient sea room, alteration of course alone may be the most effective action to avoid a close-quarters situation provided that it is made in good time, is substantial and does not result in another close-quarters situation.

(d) Action taken to avoid collision with another vessel shall be such as to result in passing at a safe distance. The effectiveness of the action shall be carefully checked until the other vessel is finally past and clear.

(e) If necessary to avoid collision or allow more time to assess the situation, a vessel shall slacken her speed or take all way off by stopping or reversing her means of propulsion.

RULE 9: *Narrow channels*

(a) A vessel proceeding along the course of a narrow channel or fairway shall keep as near to the outer limit of the channel or fairway which lies on her starboard side as is safe and practicable.

(b) A vessel of less than 20 metres in length or a sailing vessel shall not impede the passage of a vessel which can safely navigate only within a narrow channel or fairway.

(c) A vessel engaged in fishing shall not impede the passage of any other vessel navigating within a narrow channel or fairway.

(d) A vessel shall not cross a narrow channel or fairway if such crossing impedes the passage of a vessel which can safely navigate only within such channel or fairway. The latter vessel may use the sound signal prescribed in Rule 34 (d) if in doubt as to the intention of the crossing vessel.

(e) (i) In a narrow channel or fairway when overtaking can take place only if the vessel to be overtaken has to take action to permit safe passing, the vessel intending to overtake shall indicate her intention by sounding the appropriate signal prescribed in Rule 34 (c) (i). The vessel to be overtaken shall, if in agreement, sound the appropriate signal prescribed in Rule 34 (c) (ii) and take steps to permit safe passing. If in doubt she may sound the signals prescribed in Rule 34 (d).

(ii) This Rule does not relieve the overtaking vessel of her obligation under Rule 13.

(f) A vessel nearing a bend or an area of a narrow channel or fairway where other vessels may be obscured by an intervening obstruction shall navigate with particular alertness and caution and shall sound the appropriate signal prescribed in Rule 34 (e).

(g) Any vessel shall, if the circumstances of the case admit, avoid anchoring in a narrow channel.

RULE 10: *Traffic separation schemes*

(a) This Rule applies to traffic separation schemes adopted by the Organization:

(b) A vessel using a traffic separation scheme shall:

(i) proceed in the appropriate traffic lane in the general direction of traffic flow for that lane;

(ii) so far as practicable keep clear of a traffic separation line or separation zone;

(iii) normally join or leave a traffic lane at the termination of the lane, but when joining or leaving from the side shall do so at as small an angle to the general direction of traffic flow as practicable.

(c) A vessel shall so far as practicable avoid crossing traffic lanes, but if obliged to do so shall cross as nearly as practicable at right angles to the general direction of traffic flow.

(d) Inshore traffic zones shall not normally be used by through traffic which can safely use the appropriate traffic lane within the adjacent traffic separation scheme.

(e) A vessel, other than a crossing vessel, shall not normally enter a separation zone or cross a separation line except:

(i) in cases of emergency to avoid immediate danger;

(ii) to engage in fishing within a separation zone.

(f) A vessel navigating in areas near the terminations of traffic separation schemes shall do so with particular caution.

(g) A vessel shall so far as practicable avoid anchoring in a traffic separation scheme or in areas near its terminations.

(h) A vessel not using a traffic separation scheme shall avoid it by as wide a margin as is practicable.

(i) A vessel engaged in fishing shall not impede the passage of any vessel following a traffic lane.

(j) A vessel of less than 20 metres in length or a sailing vessel shall not impede the safe passage of a power-driven vessel following a traffic lane.

Section II.   Conduct of vessels in sight of one another

RULE 11: *Application*
Rules in this Section apply to vessels in sight of one another.

RULE 12: *Sailing vessels*
(a) When two sailing vessels are approaching one another, so as to involve risk of collision, one of them shall keep out of the way of the other as follows:
  (i) when each has the wind on a different side, the vessel which has the wind on the port side shall keep out of the way of the other;
  (ii) when both have the wind on the same side, the vessel which is to windward shall keep out of the way of the vessel which is to leeward;
  (iii) if a vessel with the wind on the port side sees a vessel to windward and cannot determine with certainty whether the other vessel has the wind on the port or on the starboard side, she shall keep out of the way of the other.
(b) For the purposes of this Rule the windward side shall be deemed to be the side opposite to that on which the mainsail is carried or, in the case of a square-rigged vessel, the side opposite to that on which the largest fore-and-aft sail is carried.

RULE 13: *Overtaking*
(a) Notwithstanding anything contained in the Rules of this Section any vessel overtaking any other shall keep out of the way of the vessel being overtaken.
(b) A vessel shall be deemed to be overtaking when coming up with another vessel from a direction more than 22.5 degrees abaft her beam, that is, in such a position with reference to the vessel she is overtaking, that at night she would be able to see only the sternlight of that vessel but neither of her sidelights.
(c) When a vessel is in any doubt as to whether she is overtaking another, she shall assume that this is the case and act accordingly.
(d) Any subsequent alteration of the bearing between the two vessels shall not make the overtaking vessel a crossing vessel within the meaning of these Rules or relieve her of the duty of keeping clear of the overtaken vessel until she is finally past and clear.

RULE 14: *Head-on situation*
(a) When two power-driven vessels are meeting on reciprocal or nearly reciprocal courses so as to involve risk of collision each shall alter her course to starboard so that each shall pass on the port side of the other.
(b) Such a situation shall be deemed to exist when a vessel sees the other ahead or nearly ahead and by night she could see the masthead lights of the other in a line or nearly in a line and/or both sidelights and by day she ob-

serves the corresponding aspect of the other vessel.

(c) When a vessel is in any doubt as to whether such a situation exists she shall assume that it does exist and act accordingly.

RULE 15: *Crossing situation*

When two power-driven vessels are crossing so as to involve risk of collision, the vessel which has the other on her own starboard side shall keep out of the way and shall, if the circumstances of the case admit, avoid crossing ahead of the other vessel.

RULE 16: *Action by give-way vessel*

Every vessel which is directed to keep out of the way of another vessel shall, so far as possible, take early and substantial action to keep well clear.

RULE 17: *Action by stand-on vessel*

(a) (i) Where one of two vessels is to keep out of the way the other shall keep her course and speed.

(ii) The latter vessel may however take action to avoid collision by her manoeuvre alone, as soon as it becomes apparent to her that the vessel required to keep out of the way is not taking appropriate action in compliance with these Rules.

(b) When, from any cause, the vessel required to keep her course and speed finds herself so close that collision cannot be avoided by the action of the give-way vessel alone, she shall take such action as will best aid to avoid collision.

(c) A power-driven vessel which takes action in a crossing situation in accordance with sub-paragraph (a) (ii) of this Rule to avoid collision with another power-driven vessel shall, if the circumstances of the case admit, not alter course to port for a vessel on her own port side.

(d) This Rule does not relieve the give-way vessel of her obligation to keep out of the way.

RULE 18: *Responsibilities between vessels*

Except where Rules 9, 10 and 13 otherwise require:

(a) A power-driven vessel underway shall keep out of the way of:
   (i) a vessel not under command;
   (ii) a vessel restricted in her ability to manoeuvre;
   (iii) a vessel engaged in fishing;
   (iv) a sailing vessel.

(b) A sailing vessel underway shall keep out of the way of:
   (i) a vessel not under command;
   (ii) a vessel restricted in her ability to manoeuvre;
   (iii) a vessel engaged in fishing.

(c) A vessel engaged in fishing when underway shall, so far as possible, keep out of the way of:
   (i) a vessel not under command;
   (ii) a vessel restricted in her ability to manoeuvre.

(d) (i) Any vessel other than a vessel not under command or a vessel restricted in her ability to manoeuvre shall, if the circumstances of the case admit, avoid impeding the safe passage of a vessel constrained by her draught, exhibiting the signals in Rule 28.

(ii) A vessel constrained by her draught shall navigate with particular caution having full regard to her special condition.

(e) A seaplane on the water shall, in general, keep well clear of all vessels and avoid impeding their navigation. In circumstances, however, where risk of collision exists, she shall comply with the Rules of this Part.

Section III.   Conduct of vessels in restricted visibility

RULE 19: *Conduct of vessels in restricted visibility*

(a) This Rule applies to vessels not in sight of one another when navigating in or near an area of restricted visibility.

(b) Every vessel shall proceed at a safe speed adapted to the prevailing circumstances and conditions of restricted visibility. A power-driven vessel shall have her engines ready for immediate manoeuvre.

(c) Every vessel shall have due regard to the prevailing circumstances and conditions of restricted visibility when complying with the Rules of Section I of this Part.

(d) A vessel which detects by radar alone the presence of another vessel shall determine if a close-quarters situation is developing and/or risk of collision exists. If so, she shall take avoiding action in ample time, provided that when such action consists of an alteration of course, so far as possible the following shall be avoided:
(i) an alteration of course to port for a vessel forward of the beam, other than for a vessel being overtaken;
(ii) an alteration of course towards a vessel abeam or abaft the beam.

(e) Except where it has been determined that a risk of collision does not exist, every vessel which hears apparently forward of her beam the fog signal of another vessel, or which cannot avoid a close-quarters situation with another vessel forward of her beam, shall reduce her speed to the minimum at which she can be kept on her course. She shall if necessary take all her way off and in any event navigate with extreme caution until danger of collision is over.

PART C.   LIGHTS AND SHAPES

RULE 20: *Application*

(a) Rules in this part shall be complied with in all weathers.

(b) The Rules concerning lights shall be complied with from sunset to sunrise, and during such times no other lights shall be exhibited, except such lights as cannot be mistaken for the lights specified in these Rules or do not impair their visibility or distinctive character, or interfere with the keeping of a proper look-out.

(c) The lights prescribed by these Rules shall, if carried, also be exhibited from sunrise to sunset in restricted visibility and may be exhibited in all other circumstances when it is deemed necessary.

(d) The Rules concerning shapes shall be complied with by day.

(e) The lights and shapes specified in these Rules shall comply with the provisions of Annex I to these Regulations.

RULE 21: *Definitions*

(a) "Masthead light" means a white light placed over the fore and aft centreline of the vessel showing an unbroken light over an arc of the horizon of 225 degrees and so fixed as to show the light from right ahead to 22.5 degrees abaft the beam on either side of the vessel.

(b) "Sidelights" means a green light on the starboard side and a red light on the port side each showing an unbroken light over an arc of the horizon of 112.5 degrees and so fixed as to show the light from right ahead to 22.5 degrees abaft the beam on its respective side. In a vessel of less than 20 metres in length the sidelights may be combined in one lantern carried on the fore and aft centreline of the vessel.

(c) "Sternlight" means a white light placed as nearly as practicable at the stern showing an unbroken light over an arc of the horizon of 135 degrees and so fixed as to show the light 67.5 degrees from right aft on each side of the vessel.

(d) "Towing light" means a yellow light having the same characteristics as the "sternlight" defined in paragraph (c) of this Rule.

(e) "All round light" means a light showing an unbroken light over an arc of the horizon of 360 degrees.

(f) "Flashing light" means a light flashing at regular intervals at a frequency of 120 flashes or more per minute.

RULE 22: *Visibility of lights*

The lights prescribed in these Rules shall have an intensity as specified in Section 8 of Annex I to these Regulations so as to be visible at the following minimum ranges:

(a) In vessels of 50 metres or more in length:
- a masthead light, 6 miles;
- a sidelight, 3 miles;
- a sternlight, 3 miles;
- a towing light, 3 miles;
- a white, red, green or yellow all-round light, 3 miles.

(b) In vessels of 12 metres or more in length but less than 50 metres in length:
- a masthead light, 5 miles; except that where the length of the vessel is less than 20 metres, 3 miles;
- a sidelight, 2 miles;
- a sternlight, 2 miles;
- a towing light, 2 miles;
- a white, red, green or yellow all-round light, 2 miles.

(c) In vessels of less than 12 metres in length:
- a masthead light, 2 miles;
- a sidelight, 1 mile;
- a sternlight, 2 miles;
- a towing light, 2 miles;
- a white, red, green or yellow all-round light, 2 miles.

RULE 23: *Power-driven vessels underway*

(a) A power-driven vessel underway shall exhibit:

127

(i) a masthead light forward;

(ii) a second masthead light abaft of and higher than the forward one; except that a vessel of less than 50 metres in length shall not be obliged to exhibit such light but may do so;

(iii) sidelights;

(iv) a sternlight.

(b) An air-cushion vessel when operating in the non-displacement mode shall, in addition to the lights prescribed in paragraph (a) of this Rule, exhibit an all-round flashing yellow light.

(c) A power-driven vessel of less than 7 metres in length and whose maximum speed does not exceed 7 knots may, in lieu of the lights prescribed in paragraph (a) of this Rule, exhibit an all-round white light. Such vessel shall, if practicable, also exhibit sidelights.

RULE 24: *Towing and pushing*

(a) A power-driven vessel when towing shall exhibit:

(i) instead of the light prescribed in Rule 23 (a) (i), two masthead lights forward in a vertical line. When the length of the tow, measuring from the stern of the towing vessel to the after end of the tow exceeds 200 metres, three such lights in a vertical line;

(ii) sidelights;

(iii) a sternlight;

(iv) a towing light in a vertical line above the sternlight;

(v) when the length of the tow exceeds 200 metres, a diamond shape where it can best be seen.

(b) When a pushing vessel and a vessel being pushed ahead are rigidly connected in a composite unit they shall be regarded as a power-driven vessel and exhibit the lights prescribed in Rule 23.

(c) A power-driven vessel when pushing ahead or towing alongside, except in the case of a composite unit, shall exhibit:

(i) instead of the light prescribed in Rule 23 (a) (i), two masthead lights forward in a vertical line;

(ii) sidelights;

(iii) a sternlight.

(d) A power-driven vessel to which paragraphs (a) and (c) of this Rule apply shall also comply with Rule 23 (a) (ii).

(e) A vessel or object being towed shall exhibit:

(i) sidelights;

(ii) a sternlight;

(iii) when the length of the tow exceeds 200 metres, a diamond shape where it can best be seen.

(f) Provided that any number of vessels being towed alongside or pushed in a group shall be lighted as one vessel,

(i) a vessel being pushed ahead, not being part of a composite unit, shall exhibit at the forward end, sidelights;

(ii) a vessel being towed alongside shall exhibit a sternlight and at the forward end, sidelights.

(g) Where from any sufficient cause it is impracticable for a vessel or object being towed to exhibit the lights prescribed in paragraph (e) of this Rule, all possible measures shall be taken to light the vessel or object towed or at least to indicate the presence of the unlighted vessel or object.

RULE 25: *Sailing vessels underway and vessels under oars*

(a) A sailing vessel underway shall exhibit:
  (i) sidelights;
  (ii) a sternlight.

(b) In a sailing vessel of less than 12 metres in length the lights prescribed in paragraph (a) of this Rule may be combined in one lantern carried at or near the top of the mast where it can best be seen.

(c) A sailing vessel underway may, in addition to the lights prescribed in paragraph (a) of this Rule, exhibit at or near the top of the mast, where they can best be seen, two all-round lights in a vertical line, the upper being red and the lower green, but these lights shall not be exhibited in conjunction with the combined lantern permitted by pragraph (b) of this Rule.

(d) (i) A sailing vessel of less than 7 metres in length shall, if practicable, exhibit the lights prescribed in paragraph (a) or (b) of this Rule, but if she does not, she shall have ready at hand an electric torch or lighted lantern showing a white light which shall be exhibited in sufficient time to prevent collision.

(ii) A vessel under oars may exhibit the lights prescribed in this Rule for sailing vessels, but if she does not, she shall have ready at hand an electric torch or lighted lantern showing a white light which shall be exhibited in sufficient time to prevent collision.

(e) A vessel proceeding under sail when also being propelled by machinery shall exhibit forward where it can best be seen a conical shape, apex downwards.

RULE 26: *Fishing vessels*

(a) A vessel engaged in fishing, whether underway or at anchor, shall exhibit only the lights and shapes prescribed in this Rule.

(b) A vessel when engaged in trawling, by which is meant the dragging through the water of a dredge net or other apparatus used as a fishing appliance, shall exhibit:
  (i) two all-round lights in a vertical line, the upper being green and the lower white, or a shape consisting of two cones with their apexes together in a vertical line one above the other; a vessel of less than 20 metres in length may instead of this shape exhibit a basket;
  (ii) a masthead light abaft of and higher than the all-round green light; a vessel of less than 50 metres in length shall not be obliged to exhibit such a light but may do so;
  (iii) when making way through the water, in addition to the lights prescribed in this paragraph, sidelights and a sternlight.

(c) A vessel engaged in fishing, other than trawling, shall exhibit:
  (i) two all-round lights in a vertical line, the upper one being red and the lower white, or a shape consisting of two cones with apexes together in a vertical line one above the other; a vessel of less than 20 metres in length may instead of this shape exhibit a basket;
  (ii) when there is outlying gear extending more than 150 metres horizontally from the vessel, an all-round white light or a cone apex upwards in the direction of the gear;
  (iii) when making way through the water, in addition to the lights prescribed in this paragraph, sidelights and a sternlight.

(d) A vessel engaged in fishing in close proximity to other vessels engaged in fishing may exhibit the additional signals described in Annex II to these Regulations.

(e) A vessel when not engaged in fishing shall not exhibit the lights or shapes prescribed in this Rule, but only those prescribed for a vessel of her length.

RULE 27: *Vessels not under command or restricted in their ability to manoeuvre*

(a) A vessel not under command shall exhibit:

(i) two all-round red lights in a vertical line where they can best be seen;

(ii) two balls or similar shapes in a vertical line where they can best be seen;

(iii) when making way through the water, in addition to the lights prescribed in this paragraph, sidelights and a sternlight.

(b) A vessel restricted in her ability to manoeuvre, except a vessel engaged in minesweeping operations, shall exhibit:

(i) three all-round lights in a vertical line where they can best be seen. The highest and lowest of these lights shall be red and the middle light shall be white;

(ii) three shapes in a vertical line where they can best be seen. The highest and lowest of these shapes shall be balls and the middle one a diamond;

(iii) when making way through the water, masthead lights, sidelights and a sternlight, in addition to the lights prescribed in sub-paragraph (i);

(iv) when at anchor, in addition to the lights or shapes prescribed in sub-paragraphs (i) and (ii), the lights, lights or shape prescribed in Rule 30.

(c) A vessel engaged in a towing operation such as renders her unable to deviate from her course shall, in addition to the lights or shapes prescribed in sub-paragraph **(b)** (i) and (ii) of this Rule, exhibit the lights or shape prescribed in Rule 24 **(a)**.

(d) A vessel engaged in dredging or underwater operations, when restricted in her ability to manoeuvre, shall exhibit the lights and shapes prescribed in paragraph **(b)** of this Rule and shall in addition, when an obstruction exists, exhibit:

(i) two all-round red lights or two balls in a vertical line to indicate the side on which the obstruction exists;

(ii) two all-round green lights or two diamonds in a vertical line to indicate the side on which another vessel may pass;

(iii) when making way through the water, in addition to the lights prescribed in this paragraph, masthead lights, sidelights and a sternlight;

(iv) a vessel to which this paragraph applies when at anchor shall exhibit the lights or shapes prescribed in sub-paragraphs (i) and (ii) instead of the lights or shape prescribed in Rule 30.

(e) Whenever the size of a vessel engaged in diving operations makes it impracticable to exhibit the shapes prescribed in paragraph **(d)** of this Rule, a rigid replica of the International Code flag "A" not less than 1 metre in height shall be exhibited. Measures shall be taken to ensure all-round visibility.

(f) A vessel engaged in minesweeping operations shall, in addition to the lights prescribed for the power-driven vessel in Rule 23, exhibit three all-round green lights or three balls. One of these lights or shapes shall be exhibited at or near the foremast head and one at each end of the fore yard. These lights or shapes indicate that it is dangerous for another vessel to approach closer than 1,000 metres astern or 500 metres on either side of the minesweeper.

(g) Vessels of less than 7 metres in length shall not be required to exhibit the lights prescribed in this Rule.

(h) The signals prescribed in this Rule are not signals of vessels in distress and requiring assistance. Such signals are contained in Annex IV to these Regulations.

RULE 28: *Vessels constrained by their draught*

A vessel constrained by her draught may, in addition to the lights prescribed for power-driven vessels in Rule 23, exhibit where they can best be seen three all-round red lights in a vertical line, or a cylinder.

RULE 29: *Pilot vessels*

(a) A vessel engaged on pilotage duty shall exhibit:
    (i) at or near the masthead, two all-round lights in a vertical line, the upper being white and the lower red;
    (ii) when underway, in addition, sidelights and a sternlight;
    (iii) when at anchor, in addition to the lights prescribed in sub-paragraph (i), the anchor light, lights or shape.

(b) A pilot vessel when not engaged on pilotage duty shall exhibit the lights or shapes prescribed for a similar vessel of her length.

RULE 30: *Anchored vessels and vessels aground*

(a) A vessel shall exhibit where it can best be seen:
    (i) in the fore part, an all-round white light or one ball;
    (ii) at or near the stern and at a lower level than the light prescribed in sub-paragraph (i), an all-round white light.

(b) A vessel of less than 50 metres in length may exhibit an all-round white light where it can best be seen instead of the lights prescribed in paragraph (a) of this Rule.

(c) A vessel at anchor may, and a vessel of 100 metres and more in length shall, also use the available working or equivalent lights to illuminate her decks.

(d) A vessel aground shall exhibit the lights prescribed in paragraph (a) or (b) of this Rule and in addition, where they can best be seen:
    (i) two all-round red lights in a vertical line;
    (ii) three balls in a vertical line.

(e) A vessel of less than 7 metres in length, when at anchor or aground, not in or near a narrow channel, fairway or anchorage, or where other vessels normally navigate, shall not be required to exhibit the lights or shapes prescribed in paragraphs (a), (b) or (d) of this Rule.

RULE 31: *Seaplanes*

Where it is impracticable for a seaplane to exhibit lights and shapes of the characteristics or in the positions prescribed in the Rules of this Part she shall exhibit lights and shapes as closely similar in characteristics and position as is possible.

PART D.   SOUND AND LIGHT SIGNALS

RULE 32: *Definitions*
(a) The word "whistle" means any sound signalling appliance capable of producing the prescribed blasts and which complies with the specifications in Annex III to these Regulations.
(b) The term "short blast" means a blast of about one second's duration.
(c) The term "prolonged blast" means a blast of from four to six seconds duration.

RULE 33: *Equipment for sound signals*
(a) A vessel of 12 metres or more in length shall be provided with a whistle and a bell and a vessel of 100 metres or more in length shall, in addition, be provided with a gong, the tone and sound of which cannot be confused with that of the bell. The whistle, bell and gong shall comply with the specifications in Annex III to these Regulations. The bell or gong or both may be replaced by other equipment having the same respective sound characteristics, provided that manual sounding of the required signals shall always be possible.
(b) A vessel of less than 12 metres in length shall not be obliged to carry the sound signalling appliances prescribed in paragraph (a) of this Rule but if she does not, she shall be provided with some other means of making an efficient sound signal.

RULE 34: *Manoeuvring and warning signals*
(a) When vessels are in sight of one another, a power-driven vessel underway, when manoeuvring as authorized or required by these Rules, shall indicate that manoeuvre by the following signals on her whistle:
– one short blast to mean "I am altering my course to starboard";
– two short blasts to mean "I am altering my course to port";
– three short blasts to mean "I am operating astern propulsion"
(b) Any vessel may supplement the whistle signals prescribed in paragraph (a) of this Rule by light signals, repeated as appropriate, whilst the manoeuvre is being carried out:
(i) these light signals shall have the following significance:
– one flash to mean "I am altering my course to starboard";
– two flashes to mean "I am altering my course to port";
– three flashes to mean "I am operating astern propulsion".
(ii) the duration of each flash shall be about one second, the interval between flashes shall be about one second, and the interval between successive signals shall be not less than ten seconds;
(iii) the light used for this signal shall, if fitted, be an all-round white light, visible at a minimum range of 5 miles, and shall comply with the provisions of Annex I.
(c) When in sight of one another in a narrow channel or fairway:

132

    (i) a vessel intending to overtake another shall in compliance with Rule 9 **(e)** (i) indicate her intention by the following signals on her whistle:

      – two prolonged blasts followed by one short blast to mean "I intend to overtake you on your starboard side";

      – two prolonged blasts followed by two short blasts to mean "I intend to overtake you on your port side".

    (ii) the vessel about to be overtaken when acting in accordance with Rule 9 **(e)** (i) shall indicate her agreement by the following signal on her whistle:

      – one prolonged, one short, one prolonged and one short blast, in that order.

(d) When vessels in sight of one another are approaching each other and from any cause either vessel fails to understand the intentions or actions of the other, or is in doubt whether sufficient action is being taken by the other to avoid collision, the vessel in doubt shall immediately indicate such doubt by giving at least five short and rapid blasts on the whistle. Such signal may be supplemented by a light signal of at least five short and rapid flashes.

(e) A vessel nearing a bend or an area of a channel or fairway where other vessels may be obscured by an intervening obstruction shall sound one prolonged blast. Such signal shall be answered with a prolonged blast by any approaching vessel that may be within hearing around the bend or behind the intervening obstruction.

(f) If whistles are fitted on a vessel at a distance apart of more than 100 metres, one whistle only shall be used for giving manoeuvring and warning signals.

RULE 35: *Sound signals in restricted visibility*

In or near an area of restricted visibility, whether by day or night, the signals prescribed in this Rule shall be used as follows:

(a) A power-driven vessel making way through the water shall sound at intervals of not more than 2 minutes one prolonged blast.

(b) A power-driven vessel underway but stopped and making no way through the water shall sound at intervals of not more than 2 minutes two prolonged blasts in succession with an interval of about 2 seconds between them.

(c) A vessel not under command, a vessel restricted in her ability to manoeuvre, a vessel constrained by her draught, a sailing vessel, a vessel engaged in fishing and a vessel engaged in towing or pushing another vessel shall, instead of the signals prescribed in paragraphs **(a)** or **(b)** or this Rule, sound at intervals of not more than 2 minutes three blasts in succession, namely one prolonged followed by two short blasts.

(d) A vessel towed or if more than one vessel is towed the last vessel of the tow, if manned, shall at intervals of not more than 2 minutes sound four blasts in succession, namely one prolonged followed by three short blasts. When practicable, this signal shall be made immediately after the signal made by the towing vessel.

(e) When a pushing vessel and a vessel being pushed ahead are rigidly connected in a composite unit they shall be regarded as a power-driven vessel and shall give the signals prescribed in paragraphs **(a)** or **(b)** of this Rule.

(f) A vessel at anchor shall at intervals of not more than one minute ring the bell rapidly for about 5 seconds. In a vessel of 100 metres or more in length the bell shall be sounded in the forepart of the vessel and immediately after the ringing of the bell the gong shall be sounded rapidly for about 5 seconds in the after part of the vessel. A vessel at anchor may in addition sound three blasts in succession, namely one short, one prolonged and one short blast, to give warning of her position and of the possibility of collision to an approaching vessel.

(g) A vessel aground shall give the bell signal and if required the gong signal prescribed in paragraph (f) of this Rule and shall, in addition, give three separate and distinct strokes on the bell immediately before and after the rapid ringing of the bell. A vessel aground may in addition sound an appropriate whistle signal.

(h) A vessel of less than 12 metres in length shall not be obliged to give the above-mentioned signals but, if she does not, shall make some other efficient sound signal at intervals of not more than 2 minutes.

(i) A pilot vessel when engaged on pilotage duty may in addition to the signals prescribed in paragraphs (a), (b) or (f) of this Rule sound an identity signal consisting of four short blasts.

RULE 36: *Signals to attract attention*
If necessary to attract the attention of another vessel any vessel may make light or sound signals that cannot be mistaken for any signal authorized elsewhere in these Rules, or may direct the beam of her searchlight in the direction of the danger, in such a way as not to embarrass any vessel.

RULE 37: *Distress signals*
When a vessel is in distress and requires assistance she shall use or exhibit the signals prescribed in Annex IV to these regulations.

PART E.   EXEMPTIONS

RULE 38: *Exemptions*
Any vessel (or class of vessels) provided that she complies with the requirements of the International Regulations for Preventing Collisions at Sea, 1960, the keel of which is laid or which is at a corresponding stage of construction before the entry into force of these Regulations may be exempted from compliance therewith as follows:

(a) The installation of lights with ranges prescribed in Rule 22, until four years after the date of entry into force of these Regulations.

(b) The installation of lights with colour specifications as prescribed in Section 7 of Annex I to these Regulations, until four years after the date of entry into force of these Regulations.

(c) The repositioning of lights as a result of conversion from Imperial to metric units and rounding off measurement figures, permanent exemption.

    (d) (i) The repositioning of masthead lights on vessels of less than 150 metres in length, resulting from the prescriptions of Section 3 (a) of Annex I, permanent exemption.

    (ii) The repositioning of masthead lights on vessels of 150 metres or more in length, resulting from the prescriptions of Section 3 (a) of

Annex I to these Regulations, until nine years after the date of entry into force of these Regulations.

(e) The repositioning of masthead lights resulting from the prescriptions of Section 2 (b) of Annex I, until nine years after the date of entry into force of these Regulations.

(f) The repositioning of sidelights resulting from the prescriptions of Sections 2 (g) and 3 (b) of Annex I, until nine years after the date of entry into force of these Regulations.

(g) The requirements for sound signal appliances prescribed in Annex III, until nine years after the date of entry into force of these Regulations.

ANNEX I

Positioning and technical details of lights and shapes

1. *Definition*
The term "height above the hull" means height above the uppermost continuous deck.

2. *Vertical positioning and spacing of lights*
(a) On a power-driven vessel of 20 metres or more in length the masthead lights shall be placed as follows:

    (i) the forward masthead light, or if only one masthead light is carried, then that light, at a height above the hull of not less than 6 metres, and, if the breadth of the vessel exceeds 6 metres, then at a height above the hull not less than such breadth, so however that the light need not be placed at a greater height above the hull than 12 metres;

    (ii) when two masthead lights are carried the after one shall be at least 4.5 metres vertically higher than the forward one.

(b) The vertical separation of masthead lights of power-driven vessels shall be such that in all normal conditions of trim the after light will be seen over and separate from the forward light at a distance of 1,000 metres from the stem when viewed from sea level.

(c) The masthead light of a power-driven vessel of 12 metres but less than 20 metres in length shall be placed at a height above the gunwale of not less than 2.5 metres.

(d) A power-driven vessel of less than 12 metres in length may carry the uppermost light at a height of less than 2.5 metres above the gunwale. When however a masthead light is carried in addition to sidelights and a sternlight, then such masthead light shall be carried at least 1 metre higher than the sidelights.

(e) One of the two or three masthead lights prescribed for a power-driven vessel when engaged in towing or pushing another vessel shall be placed in the same position as the forward masthead light of a power-driven vessel.

(f) In all circumstances the masthead light or lights shall be so placed as to be above and clear of all other lights and obstructions.

(g) The sidelights of a power-driven vessel shall be placed at a height above the hull not greater than three-quarters of that of the forward masthead light. They shall not be so low as to be interfered with by deck lights.

(h) The sidelights, if in a combined lantern and carried on a power-driven vessel of less than 20 metres in length, shall be placed not less than 1 metre below the masthead light.

(i) When the Rules prescribe two or three lights to be carried in a vertical line, they shall be spaced as follows:

      (i) on a vessel of 20 metres in length or more such lights shall be spaced not less than 2 metres apart, and the lowest of these lights shall, except where a towing light is required, not be less than 4 metres above the hull;

     (ii) on a vessel of less than 20 metres in length such lights shall be spaced not less than 1 metre apart and the lowest of these lights shall, except where a towing light is required, not be less than 2 metres above the gunwale;

    (iii) when three lights are carried they shall be equally spaced.

(j) The lower of the two all-round lights prescribed for a fishing vessel when engaged in fishing shall be at a height above the sidelights not less than twice the distance between the two vertical lights.

(k) The forward anchor light, when two are carried, shall not be less than 4.5 metres above the after one. On a vessel of 50 metres or more in length this forward anchor light shall not be less than 6 metres above the hull.

3. *Horizontal positioning and spacing of lights*

(a) When two masthead lights are prescribed for a power-driven vessel, the horizontal distance between them shall not be less than one-half of the length of the vessel but need not be more than 100 metres. The forward light shall be placed not more than one-quarter of the length of the vessel from the stem.

(b) On a vessel of 20 metres or more in length the sidelights shall not be placed in front of the forward masthead lights. They shall be placed at or near the side of the vessel.

4. *Details of location of direction-indicating lights for fishing vessels, dredgers and vessels engaged in underwater operations*

(a) The light indicating the direction of the outlying gear from a vessel engaged in fishing as prescribed in Rule 26 (c) (ii) shall be placed at a horizontal distance of not less than 2 metres and not more than 6 metres away from the two all-round red and white lights. This light shall be placed not higher than the all-round white light prescribed in Rule 26 (c) (i) and not lower than the sidelights.

(b) The lights and shapes on a vessel engaged in dredging or underwater operations to indicate the obstructed side and/or the side on which it is safe to pass, as prescribed in Rule 27 **(d)** (i) and (ii), shall be placed at the maximum practical horizontal distance, but in no case less than 2 metres, from the lights or shapes prescribed in Rule 27 **(b)** (i) and (ii). In no case shall the upper of these lights or shapes be at a greater height than the lower of the three lights or shapes prescribed in Rule 27 **(b)** (i) and (ii).

136

5. Screens for sidelights

The sidelights shall be fitted with inboard screens painted matt black, and meeting the requirements of Section 9 of this Annex. With a combined lantern, using a single vertical filament and a very narrow division between the green and red sections, external screens need not be fitted.

6. Shapes

(a) Shapes shall be black and of the following sizes:
  (i) a ball shall have a diameter of not less than 0.6 metre;
  (ii) a cone shall have a base diameter of not less than 0.6 metre and a height equal to its diameter;
  (iii) a cylinder shall have a diameter of at least 0.6 metre and a height of twice its diameter;
  (iv) a diamond shape shall consist of two cones as defined in (ii) above having a common base.

(b) The vertical distance between shapes shall be at least 1.5 metre.

(c) In a vessel of less than 20 metres in length shapes of lesser dimensions but commensurate with the size of the vessel may be used and the distance apart may be correspondingly reduced.

7. Colour specification of lights

The chromaticity of all navigation lights shall conform to the following standards, which lie within the boundaries of the area of the diagram specified for each colour by the International Commission on Illumination (CIE).

The boundaries of the area for each colour are given by indicating the corner co-ordinates, which are as follows:

(i) White

x	0.525	0.525	0.452	0.310	0.310	0.443
y	0.382	0.440	0.440	0.348	0.283	0.382

(ii) Green

x	0.028	0.009	0.300	0.203
y	0.385	0.723	0.511	0.356

(iii) Red

x	0.680	0.660	0.735	0.721
y	0.320	0.320	0.265	0.259

(iv) Yellow

x	0.612	0.618	0.575	0.575
y	0.382	0.382	0.425	0.406

8. Intensity of lights

(a) The minimum luminous intensity of lights shall be calculated by using the formula:

$$I = 3.43 \times 10^6 \times T \times D^2 \times K^{-D}$$

where I is luminous intensity in candelas under service conditions,
  T is threshold factor 2×10^{-7} lux,
  D is range of visibility (luminous range) of the light in nautical miles,
  K is atmospheric transmissivity.
  For prescribed lights the value of K shall be 0.8, corresponding to a meteorological visibility of approximately 13 nautical miles.

(b) A selection of figures derived from the formula is given in the following table:

Range of visibility (luminous range) of light in nautical miles D	Luminous intensity of light in candelas for K = 0.8 I
1	0.9
2	4.3
3	12
4	27
5	52
6	94

Note: The maximum luminous intensity of navigation lights should be limited to avoid undue glare.

9. *Horizontal sectors*

    (a) (i) In the forward direction, sidelights as fitted on the vessel must show the minimum required intensities. The intensities must decrease to reach practical cut-off between 1 degree and 3 degrees outside the prescribed sectors.

        (ii) For sternlights and masthead lights and at 22.5 degrees abaft the beam for sidelights, the minimum required intensities shall be maintained over the arc of the horizon up to 5 degrees within the limits of the sectors prescribed in Rule 21. From 5 degrees within the prescribed sectors the intensity may decrease by 50 per cent up to the prescribed limits; it shall decrease steadily to reach practical cut-off at not more than 5 degrees outside the prescribed limits.

    (b) All-round lights shall be so located as not to be obscured by masts, topmasts or structures within angular sectors of more than 6 degrees, except anchor lights, which need not be placed at an impracticable height above the hull.

10. *Vertical sectors*

    (a) The vertical sectors of electric lights, with the exception of lights on sailing vessels shall ensure that:

        (i) at least the required minimum intensity is maintained at all angles from 5 degrees above to 5 degrees below the horizontal;

        (ii) at least 60 per cent of the required minimum intensity is maintained from 7.5 degrees above to 7.5 degrees below the horizontal.

    (b) In the case of sailing vessels the vertical sectors of electric lights shall ensure that:

        (i) at least the required minimum intensity is maintained at all angles from 5 degrees above to 5 degrees below the horizontal;

        (ii) at least 50 per cent of the required minimum intensity is maintained from 25 degrees above to 25 degrees below the horizontal.

    (c) In the case of lights other than electric these specifications shall be met as closely as possible.

11. *Intensity of non-electric lights*

Non-electric lights shall so far as practicable comply with the minimum intensities, as specified in the Table given in Section 8 of this Annex.

12. *Manoeuvring light*

Notwithstanding the provisions of paragraph 2 (f) of this Annex the manoeuvring light described in Rule 34 (b) shall be placed in the same fore and aft vertical plane as the masthead light or lights and, where practicable, at a minimum height of 2 metres vertically above the forward masthead light, provided that it shall be carried not less than 2 metres vertically above or below the after masthead light. On a vessel where only one masthead light is carried the manoeuvring light, if fitted, shall be carried where it can best be seen, not less than 2 metres vertically apart from the masthead light.

13. *Approval*

The construction of lanterns and shapes and the installation of lanterns on board the vessel shall be to the satisfaction of the appropriate authority of the State where the vessel is registered.

ANNEX II

Additional signals
for fishing vessels fishing
in close proximity

1. *General*

The lights mentioned herein shall, if exhibited in pursuance of Rule 26 (d), be placed where they can best be seen. They shall be at least 0.9 metre apart but at a lower level than lights prescribed in Rule 26 (b) (i) and (c) (i). The lights shall be visible all round the horizon at a distance of at least 1 mile but at a lesser distance than the lights prescribed by these Rules for fishing vessels.

2. *Signals for trawlers*

(a) Vessels when engaged in trawling, whether using demersal or pelagic gear, may exhibit:

- (i) when shooting their nets:
  - two white lights in a vertical line;
- (ii) when hauling their nets:
  - one white light over one red light in a vertical line;
- (iii) when the net has come fast upon an obstruction:
  - two red lights in a vertical line.

(b) Each vessel engaged in pair trawling may exhibit:

- (i) by night, a searchlight directed forward and in the direction of the other vessel of the pair;
- (ii) when shooting or hauling their nets or when their nets have come fast upon an obstruction, the lights prescribed in 2 (a) above.

3. *Signals for purse seiners*

Vessels engaged in fishing with purse seine gear may exhibit two yellow lights in a vertical line. These lights shall flash alternately every second and with equal light and occultation duration. These lights may be exhibited only when the vessel is hampered by its fishing gear.

ANNEX III

Technical details of sound signal appliances

1. *Whistles*

(a) *Frequencies and range of audibility*

The fundamental frequency of the signal shall lie within the range 70-700 Hz.

The range of audibility of the signal from a whistle shall be determined by those frequencies, which may include the fundamental and/or one or more higher frequencies, which lie within the ranges 180-700 Hz ($\pm$ 1 per cent) and which provide the sound pressure levels specified in paragraph 1 (c) below.

(b) *Limits of fundamental frequencies*

To ensure a wide variety of whistle characteristics, the fundamental frequency of a whistle shall be between the following limits:

    (i) 70-200 Hz, for a vessel 200 metres or more in length;

    (ii) 13-350 Hz, for a vessel 75 metres but less than 200 metres in length;

    (iii) 250-700 Hz, for a vessel less than 75 metres in length.

(c) *Sound signal intensity and range of audibility*

A whistle fitted in a vessel shall provide, in the direction of maximum intensity of the whistle and at a distance of 1 metre from it, a sound pressure level in at least 1/3rd-octave band within the range of frequencies 180-700 Hz ($\pm$ 1 per cent) of not less than the appropriate figure given in the table below.

Length of vessel in metres	1/3rd-octave band level at 1 metre in dB referred to 2×10^{-5} N/m^2	Audibility range in nautical miles
200 or more	143	2
75 but less than 200	138	1.5
20 but less than 75	130	1
Less than 20	120	0.5

The range of audibility in the table above is for information and is approximately the range at which a whistle may be heard on its forward axis with 90 per cent probability in conditions of still air on board a vessel having average background noise level at the listening posts (taken to be 68 dB in the octave band centred on 250 Hz and 63 dB in the octave band centred on 500 Hz).

In practice the range at which a whistle may be heard is extremely variable and depends critically on weather conditions; the values given can be regarded as typical but under conditions of strong wind or high ambient noise level at the listening post the range may be much reduced.

(d) *Directional properties*

The sound pressure level of a directional whistle shall be not more than 4 dB below the sound pressure level on the axis at any direction in the horizontal plane within ± 45 degrees of the axis. The sound pressure level at any other direction in the horizontal plane shall be not more than 10 dB below the sound pressure level on the axis, so that the range in any direction will be at least half the range on the forward axis. The sound pressure level shall be measured in that 1/3rd-octave band which determines the audibility range.

(e) *Positioning of whistles*

When a directional whistle is to be used as the only whistle on a vessel, it shall be installed with its maximum intensity directed straight ahead.

A whistle shall be placed as high as practicable on a vessel, in order to reduce interception of the emitted sound by obstructions and also to minimize hearing damage risk to personnel. The sound pressure level of the vessel's own signal at listening posts shall not exceed 110 dB (A) and so far as practicable should not exceed 100 dB (A).

(f) *Fitting of more than one whistle*

If whistles are fitted at a distance apart of more than 100 metres, it shall be so arranged that they are not sounded simultaneously.

(g) *Combined whistle systems*

If due to the presence of obstructions the sound field of a single whistle or of one of the whistles referred to in paragraph 1 (f) above is likely to have a zone of greatly reduced signal level, it is recommended that a combined whistle system be fitted so as to overcome this reduction. For the purposes of the Rules a combined whistle system is to be regarded as a single whistle. The whistles of a combined system shall be located at a distance apart of not more than 100 metres and arranged to be sounded simultaneously. The frequency of any one whistle shall differ from those of the others by at least 10 Hz.

2. *Bell or gong*

(a) *Intensity of signal*

A bell or gong, or other device having similar sound characteristics shall produce a sound pressure levelof not less than 110 dB at 1 metre.

(b) *Construction*

Bells and gongs shall be made of corrosion-resistant material and designed to give a clear tone. The diameter of the mouth of the bell shall be not less than 300 mm. for vessels of more than 20 metres in length, and shall be not less than 200 mm. for vessels of 12 to 20 metres in length. Where practicable, a power-driven bell striker is recommended to ensure constant force but manual operation shall be possible. The mass of the striker shall be not less than 3 per cent of the mass of the bell.

3. *Approval*

The construction of sound signal appliances, their performance and their installation on board the vessel shall be to the satisfaction of the appropriate authority of the State where the vessel is registered.

ANNEX IV

Distress signals

1. The following signals, used or exhibited either together or separately, indicate distress and need of assistance:
> (a) a gun or other explosive signal fired at intervals of about a minute;
> (b) a continuous sounding with any fog-signalling apparatus;
> (c) rockets or shells, throwing red stars fired one at a time at short intervals;
> (d) a signal made by radiotelegraphy or by any other signalling method consisting of the group $\cdots - - - \cdots$ (SOS) in the Morse Code;
> (e) a signal sent by radiotelephony consisting of the spoken word "Mayday";
> (f) the International Code Signal of distress indicated by N.C.;
> (g) a signal consisting of a square flag having above or below it a ball or anything resembling a ball;
> (h) flames on the vessel (as from a burning tar barrel, oil barrel, etc.);
> (i) a rocket parachute flare or a hand flare showing a red light;
> (j) a smoke signal giving off orange-coloured smoke;
> (k) slowly and repeatedly raising and lowering arms outstretched to each side;
> (l) the radiotelegraph alarm signal;
> (m) the radiotelephone alarm signal;
> (n) signals transmitted by emergency position-indicating radio beacons.

2. The use or exhibition of any of the foregoing signals except for the purpose of indicating distress and need of assistance and the use of other signals which may be confused with any of the above signals is prohibited.

3. Attention is drawn to the relevant sections of the International Code of Signals, the Merchant Ship Search and Rescue Manual and the following signals:
> (a) a piece of orange-coloured canvas with either a black square and circle or other appropriate symbol (for identification from the air);
> (b) a dye marker.